Rosalía de Castro

Also by Michael Smith from Shearsman Books:

Poetry
The Purpose of the Gift: Selected Poems

Poetry in Translation
Maldon & Other Translations
Gustavo Adolof Bécquer: Collected Poems (Rimas)

Edited & translated with Valentino Gianuzzi:

The Complete Poems of César Vallejo in Three Volumes:
  The Black Heralds & Other Early Poems
  Trilce
  Complete Later Poems 1923-1938

César Vallejo: Selected Poems

Selected Poems

Rosalía de Castro

Edited and translated by
Michael Smith

Shearsman Books
Exeter

First published in the United Kingdom in 2007 by
Shearsman Books Ltd
58 Velwell Road
Exeter EX4 4LD

www.shearsman.com

ISBN-13 978-1-905700-44-8

ISBN-10 1-905700-44-X

Translations copyright © Michael Smith, 2007.

The right of Michael Smith to be identified as the author of these translations and introductions has been asserted by him in accordance with the Copyrights, Designs and Patents Act of 1988. All rights reserved. No part of this publication may be reproduced, stored in a retrieval system, transmitted in any form or by any means, electronic, mechanical, photocopying, recording or otherwise, without the prior permission of the publisher.

Acknowledgements
The publisher and translator thank the Xunta de Galicia (the Regional Government of Galicia) for their financial assistance with the translation and publication of this book.

Contents

Biography	9
Introduction	11
Acknowledgements	13

from *A mi madre*

The hot season now over	17
Wandering, fugitive, mysterious,	17
Clothes and hair loose to the wind	19
Now all light grew dark in the sky	19
But . . . what a strident and magical howl	21
Where the erect cypress rises,	21
And must I calmly enjoy	23
God forbid I should forget you	23

from *Cantares gallegos*

When I hear you toll	25
There in the early morning	27
In the quiet evening	27
Every star, its diamond	29
The wind blows, the river flows	31

from *Follas novas*

A Few Words from the Author	32
I well know there is nothing	39
As the clouds	39
You will say about these verses, and it's true	41
What's happening around me?	41
New leaves! the name you bear	43
Some people say, My country!	43
Once I had a nail	45
When one is very, very lucky	47
Today or tomorrow, who can say when?	49
That buzz of songs and laughter	51
Now neither rancour nor disdain	53
Quiet!	53

Goodbye!	55
In the Cathedral	57
No Charge	61
Weeping I thought each night	63
Who Does Not Lament?	65
Sea, with your unfathomed waters	67
Dig fast, dig	67
When I think you are gone	69
Happiness is Treacherous	71
Tick-tock, tick-tock, in the silent night	73
Flow, serene crystal waves	75
How placid the sparkling!	77
Padrón! . . . Padrón!	79

from **En las orillas del Sar**

Some, very high	85
You sense the sweet and fragrant	87
Now passions sleep in their tomb	87
A gentle river, a narrow lane	89
Thirsting on the beach, the sands	89
Soul, in flight from yourself	91
Along the ancient road	91
Some smeared him with slander	93
In their prison of thorns and roses	95
It was the last night	97
White road, old road	99
It seems that, behind proud Miranda, they still loom	101
The moon, silent and, as always, pale	101
The saddest shadow, indefinable and vague	103
When the harsh Northwind blows	103
Some say plants don't speak, nor fountains, nor birds	105
Black-winged thoughts! flee, flee in harass-ridden	107
The hearts of some creatures	109
The word and the idea . . . There's an abyss	109
"The dead go fast"	111
In this world's endless	111

The Bells	113
High up the ravens croaked	115
Justice of men, I seek you out	115
As from the high summit	117
Doubtless, he wasn't born to love, no	119
Although they may not achieve glory	119
Hour after hour, day after day	121
The day was mild	123
Women Writers	126

Brief Biography: Some Names and Dates

María Rosalía Rita was born on the 24 of February, 1837, in Camiño Novo, outside Santiago de Compostela in Galicia. Her parents were José Martínez Viojo (1798-1870), a priest in the Santiago Cathedral, and María Teresa de la Cruz de Castro y Abadía (1804-1862). Her mother came from an established bourgeois family. Until she was seven, Rosalía lived with two paternal aunts in a village close to Santiago. The illegitimacy of her birth played a considerable role in the development of Rosalía's character. In the Spain of her time, not only was it a great disgrace to be illegitimate, but, worse still, was to be known as a 'sacrilegious' child, that is to say, the offspring of a cleric. By law, this offspring could not live with either parent, nor could it take their surname. Some of Rosalía's fictions betray sharply her craving for a father figure.

It was only sometime in the late 1840s, when her mother's father died, that Rosalía went to live with her mother in Padrón, and in 1850 mother and daughter went to live in Santiago. There Rosalía learnt something of music and drawing.

In September of 1853 she took part at Muxía in the *romería de Nosa Señora da Barca*, a pilgrimage with some peculiar traits: thus the belief that a stone ship brought to this shore the effigy of Our Lady, invoked since by seamen. The sanctuary rises on the very waterfront, so that even waves of middling height hit the entrance. The ritual includes, for men, treading to a balance (*avalar*) on a giant rocking slab, so they are ascertained of good health; for women, to walk across the cavity in a tall rock (the *cadrís* or hip rock), so they become fertile. Here, however, Rosalía fell sick with typhus. In the winter of this year, known as the *Año del Hambre*, which was one of the many great famines to affect Galicia, Rosalía witnessed that horrendous spectacle of thousands of Galician peasants begging alms in the streets of Santiago. It would not be the first of such scenes she would witness within the course of her life, to her great distress and with deep compassion.

In 1854 in the Liceo de la Juventud Rosalía took a principal role in a drama, and there, among others, she met her future husband, Miguel Murguía. In April 1856 Rosalía went to live in Madrid with one of her mother's cousins. Her first small collection of poems, *La flor*, was published in 1857 and it received a warm review from Murguía, who was then working as a journalist. Her relationship with Murguía was to lead to their marriage in 1858. For the next few years Rosalía and her husband lived in various places, including Santiago, Madrid, Lestrove, A Coruña. In Santiago in 1859 her first child, Alejandra, was born. This daughter would live until 1937, and it was she who destroyed Rosalía's manuscript remains, as requested by her mother. In 1860 in Santiago, Rosalía took part in an historical drama by Juan de Ariza. In 1861 her first poem in Galician was published.

Rosalía's mother died in June of 1862. Despite its inauspicious beginning, the relationship between Rosalía and her mother was extremely deep, as can be seen from the poems written by Rosalía after her mother's death. There is never the slightest hint of blame for her mother's early abandonment of her: she knew all too well the circumstances that had led to it.

In 1863, Rosalía's *Cantares gallegos* appeared and was a major contribution towards the revival of Galician literature after centuries of non-existence, indeed since the Middle Ages. In 1858 Murguía became Government archivist for the archive of Simancas, in the province of Valladolid; later, in 1870, he became Head of the General Archive of Galicia. In 1871 Rosalía gave birth to twins, Gala and Ovidio, and in 1873 another daughter, Amara. A son, Alejandro, was born on March 20, 1875, and died the following year on November 1876 as the result of a fall from a table, and in 1877 a last child, Valentina, was stillborn.

Rosalía spent her final years in Padrón. In 1885, the cancer from which she had been suffering worsened. Knowing that her death was near, she moved to Carril (on the estuary of the Arosa) so that she could have her last views of the sea before her death on July 15, 1885.

Introduction

It is not my intention to write a detailed introduction to the poetry of Rosalía de Castro. That is more properly the work of a scholarly hispanist than a humble translator such as myself. But before adding my pennyworth to the understanding and appreciation of the work of the Galician poet, a little might usefully be said about her place in Spanish poetry.

For centuries, Galicia was an economically backward region of Spain. Over-populated, the region suffered from dreadful exploitation of its peasantry by feudal landlordism. Emigration or starvation was often the only choice that faced the majority of the Galician peasantry. Their different language and their poverty even in a poverty-ridden country as the Spain of the time, marked out Galician peasants as the lowest of the low in the class structure of Spanish society. Galician had ceased to be a written language since the medieval *cántigas de amigo*. Early in the 19th century, efforts were made by some individuals to renew Galician culture and recover its written language. This situation is very similar, in cause and effect, to the revival of native Irish culture in the early 19th century. Rosalía was a major participant in this revival.

Her *Cantares gallegos* (*Galician Songs*, 1863) gave the Galician peasant, usually illiterate, a new sense of self-respect. The poems in this book, using popular, traditional forms, were taken up by the Galician peasantry with huge pleasure and pride. In general the poems celebrate the Galician countryside, the customs of the people and express many of the region's endemic frustrations. It was as if the voice of the people, of a whole ancient community, had at last found some satisfaction in having its life articulated with dignity and understanding.

Rosalía's next book of poems in Galician, *Follas novas* (*New Leaves*, 1880), was not so happily received by the Galicians. Whereas her *Cantares gallegos* has a collective voice, *Follas novas* is more personal, more individual. Still, the folkloristic voice is not altogether lacking, but rather more muted.

Finally, in 1884, Rosalía abandoned Galician and wrote her last poems in Castilian. *En las orillas del Sar* (*By the Banks of the Sar*) is a deeply personal book that at the same time concerns itself with the communal themes Rosalía considered equally hers.

It has only been in recent times that the poetry of Rosalía de Castro has emerged from its traditional categorization as folkloristic and therefore limited in interest. Even an admirer of her poetry such as Unamuno scarcely saw her work as more than the soulful expression of 'that poor villager – it was always what Rosalía was – *carrying the plain of Padrón in her soul*' (aquella pobre aldeana – siempre lo fue Rosalia – *llevando a la vega de Padrón en el alma*). Even more condescending are the words of Valle-Inclán who saw Rosalía merely as a nostalgic peasant woman who laments in an eternal monotone moan (*la campesina nostálgica que llora en una eternal queja monocorde*). Menéndez y Pelayo does not even mention her in his writings; Clarín ignores her altogether; Valera omits her from his mediocre anthology of women's poetry.

On the other hand, Rosalía has been praised by Lorca, and Juan Ramón Jiménez was perceptive enough to see the affinity of her poetry to that of Antonio Machado. Luis Cernuda also praised her work.

The trouble here, it seems to me, is that Rosalía made her reputation as a provincial, folkloristic poet with her *Cantares gallegos*, and she continued to be read as such, even by cultivated critics such as Unamuno. Indeed, her decision to write her last book of poems in Castilian was perceived by many as an act of betrayal to her 'true' métier of Galician: as if to say, she should have stayed with what she was good at . . . the typical macho criticism of women writers until recent times.

The argument I wish to put forward here is that Rosalía de Castro's poetry develops from the articulation of collective experience to a deeply and intimately personal expression of what was once called existential angst. She is not a Spanish Emily Dickinson whose New England Puritan background produced an isolated consciousness, despite its communal trappings. Rosalía's experience, in its most intimate nature, is always deeply imbued with a communal sense usually lacking in the North American poet. This distinction, of course, is not a matter of better or worse, but merely of difference.

As regards my method of translation, it will be immediately obvious that I have not 'versified' Rosalía's poems, hoping thereby to avoid the debilitation of paraphrase and padding. Instead, I have attempted to achieve rhythms appropriate to each poem while at the same time staying 'faithful' to my originals. How successful this tactic has been is for others to decide.

Acknowledgements

The original text used for the following translations is mainly that of that of the *Obras completas* in two volumes, edited by Marina Mayoral (Madrid: Turner, Biblioteca Castro, 1993). I chose to stay with this, despite its shortcomings — it has no notes or index of first lines — in order to avoid the complexities of orthography and textuality that belong to the area of scholarship. Three poems, 'Hora tras hora', 'Era apacible el día' and 'Aunque no alcancen gloria', were not chosen by Rosalía herself for the first edition of *En las orillas del Sar* (1884) but were added to a second edition by her husband Manuel Murguía: he included an additional eleven poems, and the justification for their inclusion has been the subject of much debate by hispanists. I include three of them here because I like them as poems and because we know for certain that they were written by Rosalía.

My longtime friend, Luis Huerga, who disdains compliments, was enormously helpful in translating these poems. Without his constant assistance, this book would not have happened.

I owe a very special thanks to two Galician friends, José Manual Estévez Saá and Margarita Estévez Saá, for their incredibly generous and unstinting help in checking my English translations, supplying many useful suggestions and over-seeing my Galician and Castilian texts. It goes without saying, however, that they should not be held responsible for any shortcomings of my own.

Some of the editions we have consulted, besides some web pages, are:

Rosalía de Castro, *Poesías: Cantares gallegos, Follas novas, En las orillas del Sar*. Vigo: Patronato Rosalía de Castro, 1976.
Rosalía de Castro, *A mi madre*. Padrón: Patronato Rosalía de Castro, 1995.
Rosalía de Castro, *Airiños, airiños, aires: antología bilingüe de sus mejores poemas en gallego*. Sel y trad. Rodolfo Alonso. Rosario, Argentina: Ameghino, 1997.
Rosalía de Castro, *Cantares gallegos*. Ed. Ricardo Carballo Calero. Madrid: Cátedra, 1989
Rosalía de Castro, *Cantares gallegos*. Vigo: Galaxia, 1990
Rosalía de Castro, *En las orillas del Sar*. A Coruña: La Voz de Galicia, 2004
Rosalía de Castro, *Follas novas*. Eds. Marina Mayoral y Blanca Roig. Vigo: Edicións Xerais de Galicia, 2000.
Rosalía de Castro, *Follas novas*. Eds. Henrique Monteagudo y Dolores Vilavedra. Vigo: Galaxia, 1993.
Rosalía de Castro, *Follas novas: Antología*. Trad. José Hierro. Valencia: Federico Domenech, 2001.

I also wish to thank my friend Luis Ingelmo for his generous assistance with the Castilian poems in this book. I was helped with my translations of the Galician poems by literal translations into Spanish made for me by some Spanish friends.

Note: I have included two prose pieces by Rosalía for the light they throw on her difficulties as a woman writer in the Spain of her time, and also for some of her ideas about writing.

I wish to dedicate this book to my daughter Lorna who was among the first to encourage me with its translation.

de A mi madre (1863)

I

Ya pasó la estación de los calores,
y lleno el rostro de áspera fiereza,
sobre los restos de las mustias flores,
asoma el crudo invierno su cabeza.

Pero el azul del claro firmamento
tiende sus alas de color sombrío,
cual en torno de un casto pensamiento
sus alas tiende un pensamiento impío.

Y gime el bosque, y el torrente brama,
y la hoja seca, en lodo convertida,
dale llorosa al céfiro a quien ama
la postrera y doliente despedida.

II

Errantes, fugitivas, misteriosas,
tienden las nubes presuroso el vuelo,
no como un tiempo, cándidas y hermosas,
sí llenas de amargura y desconsuelo.

Más allá . . . más allá . . . siempre adelante,
prosiguen sin descanso su carrera,
bañado en llanto el pálido semblante
con que riegan el bosque y la pradera.

Que enojada la mar donde se miran
y oscurecido el sol que las amó,
sólo saben decir cuando suspiran:
«Todo para nosotras acabó.»

from *To My Mother* (1863)

I

The hot season now over,
rough, fierce, harsh-faced winter
lifts its head above what's left
of the withered flowers.

Now the blue of a clear sky
spreads its wings of dismal hue,
like an impious thought
over a chaste mind.

And the wood groans, and the torrent roars,
and the dry leaf, turned to mush,
gives its beloved zephyr
a last and grieving goodbye.

II

Wandering, fugitive, mysterious,
the clouds take their swift flight,
not, as once, artless and fair,
but laden with spite and grief.

Further on . . . further on . . . , always forward,
tirelessly they pursue their course,
their pale visage bathed in those tears
that drench the wood and the meadow.

How angry the sea where they're mirrored,
and darkened the sun that loved them,
they can only say while sighing:
'For us things are ended.'

III

Suelto el ropaje y la melena al viento,
cual se agrupan en torno de la luna . . .
locas en incesante movimiento,
remedan el vaivén de la fortuna.

Pasan, vuelven y corren desatadas,
hijas del aire en forma caprichosa,
al viento de la noche abandonadas
en la profunda oscuridad medrosa.

Tal en mi triste corazón inquietas,
mis locas esperanzas se agitaron,
y a un débil hilo de placer sujetas,
locas . . . , locas también se quebrantaron.

IV

Ya toda luz se oscureció en el cielo,
cubriéndose de luto las estrellas,
y de luto también se cubrió el suelo,
entre brisas, gemidos y querellas.

Todo en profunda noche adormecido,
sólo el rumor del huracán se siente,
y se parece su áspero silbido
al silbido feroz de una serpiente.

¡Cuán tenebrosa noche se presenta! . . .
Mas al abrigo de amoroso techo,
grato es pensar que la hórrida tormenta
no ha de agitar la colcha de mi lecho.

III

Clothes and hair loose to the wind,
as they gather around the moon;
crazy in incessant movement
they mimic fortune's to-and-fro.

They pass, return and race unbound,
the air's children in fickle form,
abandoned to the wind of night
in the deep and awesome dark.

So, in my sorrowing heart, restless
and wild expectations stirred,
and held by pleasure's feeble thread,
wild . . . , wild, they also broke.

IV

Now all light grew dark in the sky,
enveloping the stars in mourning,
and mourning, too, covered the earth,
among breezes, groans and gripes.

All things in deep night's drowsiness,
only the whirlwind's blast is heard,
and its rasping whistle mimics
a serpent's vicious hiss.

What a dismal night comes on!
But under the shelter of a loving roof,
it's pleasant to think the horrid storm
will never stir my bed's counterpane.

V

Mas . . . ¿qué estridente y mágico alarido
la ronca voz de la tormenta trae?
Triste . . . vago . . . constante y dolorido,
cual fuego ardiente, en mis entrañas cae.

Cae y ahuyenta de mi lecho el sueño . . .
¡Ah¡ ¿Cómo he de dormir? . . . Locura fuera,
fuera locura y temerario empeño
que con gemidos tales me durmiera.

¡Ah¡ ¿Cómo he de dormir? Ese lamento,
ese grito de angustia que percibo,
esa expresión de amargo sufrimiento
no pertenece al mundo en que yo vivo.

VI

Donde el ciprés erguido se levanta,
allá en lejana habitación sombría,
que al más osado de la tierra espanta,
sola duerme la dulce madre mía.

Más helado es su lecho que la nieve,
más negro y hondo que caverna oscura,
y el euro altivo que sus antros mueve,
sacia su furia en él, con saña dura.

¡Ah!, de dolientes sauces rodeada,
de dura hierba y ásperas ortigas,
¡cuál serás, madre, en tu dormir turbada
por vaporosas sombras enemigas!

V

But . . . what a strident and magical howl
the storm's raucous voice brings?
Sad . . . vague . . . constant and aggrieved,
it falls, burning like fire, inside me.

It falls and chases sleep far from my bed . . .
Ah! How could I sleep? . . . It would be madness,
madness and foolhardy to attempt
going to sleep amid such shrieks.

How, indeed, could I sleep? That lament,
that shout of anguish I perceive,
that expression of bitter distress
does not belong to the world I live in.

VI

Where the erect cypress rises,
in a distant, dark room
that awes the boldest on the earth,
solitary, my gentle mother sleeps.

Her bed is icier than snow,
blacker and deeper than a dark cave,
the haughty breath that stirs its hollows
slakes its wrath with wanton rage.

Ah! Surrounded by gloomy willows,
by rough nettles and hard grass,
what vague, hostile shadows,
Mother, may trouble your rest?

VII

¿Y yo tranquila, he de gozar en tanto
de blando sueño y lecho cariñoso,
mientras herida de mortal espanto
moras en el profundo tenebroso?

¿Llegará a tanto el insensible olvido? . . .
¿La ingratitud del hombre a tanto alcanza,
que entre uno y otro lazo desunido
ceda siempre al vaivén de la mudanza?

¡Odioso y torpe proceder de un hijo
a quien la dulce madre en su agonía,
con besos y caricias le bendijo
olvidando el dolor por que moría!

VIII

Nunca permita Dios que yo te olvide,
mi santa, mi amorosa compañera;
nunca permita Dios que yo te olvide,
aunque por tanto recordarte muera.

Venga hacia mí tu imagen tan amada
y hábleme al alma en su lenguaje mudo,
ya en la serena noche y reposada,
ya en la que es parto del invierno crudo.

Y que en tu aislado apartamiento fiero,
tan ajeno del hombre y su locura,
velen me llanto y mi dolor primero
al lado de tu humilde sepultura.

VII

And must I calmly enjoy
an easy sleep and a loving bed,
while you, struck by death's fright,
dwell in the dark's depth?

Will oblivion reach that far?
Is man's ingratitude so great,
it always yields, as bonds slacken,
to the to-and-fro of change?

A child's base and odious deed,
whom the dear mother, in her throes,
blest with kisses and caresses,
forgetful of the pain she died in!

VIII

God forbid I should forget you,
my saint, my loving companion;
God forbid I should forget you,
though I should die, remembering you!

Let your dear image come to me
and speak to my soul in its mute tongue,
or in a serene and restful night,
or in a harsh night winter brings.

And in your wild, forlorn isolation,
alien to man and his folly,
let my weeping and my sorrow
keep vigil at your humble grave.

de *Cantares gallegos* (1868)

Campanas de Bastabales,
cando vos oio tocar,
mórrome de soidades.

I

Cando vos oio tocar,
campaniñas, campaniñas,
sin querer torno a chorar.

Cando de lonxe vos oio,
penso que por min chamades,
e das entrañas me doio.

Dóiome de dor ferida,
que antes tiña vida enteira,
i hoxe teño, media vida.

Sólo media me deixaron
os que de aló me trouxeron,
os que de aló me roubaron.

Non me roubaron, traidores,
¡ai!, uns amores toliños,
¡ai!, uns toliños amores.

Que os amores xa fuxiron,
as soidades viñeron . . .
de pena me consumiron.

from *Galician Songs* (1868)

Bells of Bastabales,
when I hear you toll,
of longing I die.

I

When I hear you toll,
little bells, little bells,
I can't help but cry.

When I hear you afar,
I think it's me you call,
and heartache conquers me.

Grief-stricken I hurt:
for I who had a full life,
now have half a life.

Half a life they've left me,
those who brought me here,
those who stole me thence.

Traitors, they didn't rob me,
ah, of some mad loves,
ah, of loves so mad!

Loves now are gone,
solitudes came instead . . .
and devoured me with grief.

II

   Aló pola mañanciña
subo enriba dos outeiros,
lixeiriña, lixeiriña.

   Como unha craba lixeira,
para oír das campaniñas
a batalada primeira.

   A primeira da alborada
que me traen os airiños
por me ver máis consolada.

   Por me ver menos chorosa,
nas súas alas ma traen
rebuldeira e queixumbrosa.

   Queixumbrosa e retembrando
por antre verde espesura,
por antre verde arborado.

   E pola verde pradeira,
por riba da veiga llana,
rebuldeira e rebuldeira.

III

   Paseniño, paseniño,
vou pola tarde calada,
 de Bastabales camiño.

   Camiño do meu contento;
i en tanto o sol non se esconde,
nunha pedriña me sento.

II

    There in the early morning
I climb up the hills,
nimbly, nimbly.

    Nimble as a goat,
to hear the first peal
of the dear bells.

    The first dawn peal
the airs bring me,
to see me cheer up.

    To see me less mournful,
they bring it on their wings,
playful and plaintive.

    Plaintive and trembling
amid the green thicket,
amid the green woodland.

    Over the green meadow,
across the smooth dale,
playful, playful.

III

    In the quiet evening,
I'm slowly, slowly,
on my way to Bastabales.

    The way of my contentment;
and before the sun sinks,
I sit down on a little stone.

E sentada estou mirando,
como a lúa vai saíndo,
como o sol se vai deitando.

Cal se deita, cal se esconde,
mentras tanto corre a lúa
sin saberse para donde.

Para donde vai tan soia,
sin que aos tristes que a miramos
nin nos fale, nin nos oia.

Que si oíra e nos falara,
moitas cousas lle dixera,
moitas cousas lle contara.

IV

Cada estrela, o seu diamante;
cada nube, branca pruma;
triste a lúa marcha diante.

Diante marcha crarexando,
veigas, prados, montes, ríos,
donde o día vai faltando.

Falta o día, e noite escura,
baixa, baixa, pouco a pouco,
por montañas de verdura.

De verdura e de follaxe,
salpicada de fontiñas
baixo a sombra do ramaxe.

And seated I stay to watch
how the moon emerges,
and how the sun sets.

How the sun sets and hides,
while the moon is gliding
to where no one knows.

Where she goes so lonely,
not speaking or listening
to us, sad and gazing.

Were she to listen or speak,
I would tell her many things,
I would relate many tales.

IV

Every star, its diamond;
every cloud, a white feather;
the sad moon moves ahead.

Ahead she moves brightening
plains, meadows, mountains, rivers,
where daylight slowly fades.

The day fails and dark night
descends, descends, gradually,
down the green mountains.

Green and foliaged mountain
sprinkled with little springs
under the branches' shade.

Do ramaxe donde cantan
paxariños piadores
que ca aurora se levantan.

Que ca noite se adormecen
para que canten os grillos
que cas sombras aparecen.

V

Corre o vento, o río pasa;
corren nubes, nubes corren
camiño da miña casa.

Miña casa, meu abrigo;
vanse todos, eu me quedo
sin compaña, nin amigo.

Eu me quedo contemprando
as laradas das casiñas
por quen vivo suspirando.

....

Ven a noite . . . , morre o día,
as campanas tocan lonxe
o tocar da *Ave María*.

Elas tocan pra que rece;
eu non rezo, que os saloucos
afogándome parece
que por min tén que rezar.
Campanas de Bastabales,
cando vos oio tocar,
mórrome de soidades.

Branches full of song
of small chirping birds
that rise up with dawn,

   that go to sleep at night
yielding to the crickets' song
that sounds loud in the darkness.

V

   The wind blows, the river flows;
the clouds drift, the clouds drift on,
and I make my way home.

   My home, my shelter:
all depart, but I stay, bereft
of companion or friend.

   I stay, intent upon
the cottage hearths
for which I live in longing.

....

   Night comes on . . . , day expires,
far off the bells toll
the *Ave Maria*.

   They toll for me to pray;
but I do not pray:
it's as if, in my stead,
my choking sobs prayed.
*Bells of Bastabales,
when I hear you toll,
of longing I die.*

from *Follas novas* (1880)

A Few Words from the Author

These verses were kept back, I may well have thought forever, justly condemned by their own condition to eternal oblivion, when, not without real pain, old commitments obliged me to bring them together much too quickly, to put them in order and give them to the printer. This was not indeed what I wanted, but there was no way out of it: I had to content myself with the duress of the circumstances that ordered it. 'Let them go, these poor verses of mine, the result of my sadness,' I said then. 'Let them go and take their chances. Let what by its nature is a dead being's dead product, go among the living.' So they went off I didn't know where nor did I care to know why.

More than ten years passed — an almost fabulous time span, judging by the speed of today's living — since most of these verses were written, the hardships of my unsettled life, and an ever failing health preventing my weary eyes and worn-out spirit from resting on them. Reading them again, I saw very clearly how incomplete and poor this poetic work of mine was, how lacking in anything of value, rather one more book, with no other merit than its steady doleful tenor, to be held by some, not unjustly, as tiresome and monotonous. But things must be as circumstances dictate, and if I cannot ever escape from my unhappiness, less so can my verses. Written in the desert of Castile, thought out and pondered on in the solitudes of Nature and of my heart, awkward offspring of the hours of illness and separation, they reflect, perhaps with too much sincerity, now the state of my spirit, now my natural disposition (not in vain am I a woman) to feel others' sorrow as my own. Ah, sadness, muse of our time, knows me well, has known for years, looks on me as its own, is another like me, does not leave me a moment, not if willing to tell of things today in the air and in one's heart. My madness! Did I say in the air? Even in my heart, but outside it? Truly, what can happen in one that doesn't happen in all? In me and in everyone! In my soul and in that of others! . . . But should it be said I think myself inspired, or that I pretend to have written what some call a crucial book? No. I neither wanted it nor did my strength stretch that far. It's true, grave things in plenty are abroad; they are easily recognised and even discussed; but I am a woman, and women are scarcely allowed, in their feminine frankness, to guess at them and see them go by. We are a harp of only two strings: imagination and feeling: in the everlasting honeycomb we work deep within, there's just honey, sweet or sweeter, of pure or purer fragrance, yet always honey, nothing but honey. For if the problems that keep busy the greatest minds have anything at all to do with us, it is inasmuch as those who share and bear at one with us the burden of life cannot hide from us all their sadness and disheartedness. It suits them to see the wounds and sound them and seek a remedy; it suits us to help support them, more with quiet deeds than with words and fuss. A woman's thought is gentle; like butterflies, we love flying from rose to rose, over things that are gentle as well: the tough work of meditating wasn't made for us. When we engage in it, unknown to us it gets tinged with our innate weakness; and if it is easy for us to deceive frivolous and unaccustomed spirits, it isn't so with men of study and reflection, who then realise that below the clear stream of form, only the insubstantial sludge of triviality is met. And in the domains of speculation, as in those of art, nothing is more idle and ruinous than the trivial. I steadily flee it with all my strength; and so I wouldn't incur such great sin, I never tried to exceed the limits of the simple poetry one may find in a happy expression, a fortunate idea; that nameless thing that moves straight as an arrow, pierces our flesh, makes us shudder and resounds in the grief-stricken soul like another ah! responding to the drawn-out lament the Earth's pangs raise in us.

    Having said that, must I add that, in a way, this book of mine is not the offspring of the same inspiration that produced *Cantares gallegos*? I need not, I think. The latter is a product of my days of hope and youth. Anyone can see it has something of the freshness peculiar to the start of life. The present book, however, written as it were in banishment from everywhere, cannot have, even wanting to, the charm that the innocence of first impressions lends: for the sun of life, that illumining the world we dwell in, does not shine at dawn as it does when, sadly, it is about to set, veiled by the clouds of late autumn.

On the other hand, in the *Cantares*, Galicia was the topic, the entire soul, while in the present book it is often just the occasion, even if always the background of the picture: for if the spirit cannot except by death shed its bodily coil, less so can the poet avoid the way in which he lives and the nature of what surrounds him; being a stranger to one's time is ceasing to render, albeit unawares, the eternal and whining lament that today all lips exhale. So out of my book's contents, I don't know how much is sorrow, mine or indeed that of others, for I may well hold the all as my own, those accustomed to misfortune coming to count as their own anything afflicting others. This is so to such an extent that in this new book of mine I've given preference, over poems one could call personal, to those which, with greater or lesser skill, tell of the tribulations of the many about me I've long seen suffering, first one, then another, in divers ways. And there is so much suffering in this dear Galician land! Whole books could be written to tell of the eternal misfortune that afflicts our villagers and sailors, the unique and true working people of our country. I saw and felt their sufferings as if these were my own; but what always moved me, and hence could not but have an echo in my poetry, were the innumerable worries of our womenfolk: creatures who love their own and others, full of feeling, as strong in body as they are gentle of heart, while unlucky to a degree, one might say they were born only to shoulder the many hardships that afflict the weakest and most simple of humanity. In the fields, their share equals that of their husbands; at home they courageously assume the burdens of motherhood, the house chores, the trials of poverty. Alone almost all the time, having to work with no aid from dawn to dusk for their poor living and that of their children, looking perhaps as well after an ailing parent: they seem condemned to find no rest except in the grave.

Emigration and the King constantly rob them of a lover, brother, husband, support of an almost always numerous family; and thus abandoned, lamenting their desertion, they are condemned to a bitter life among the uncertainties of hope, the blackness of solitude and the suffering of perennial misery. That's what saddens them most, their menfolk all going away: some because they are taken, others moved by example, or out of necessity, or through blind greed however excusable, all are made to flee the hearth dear to the one they loved, the wife now mother and the numerous children, so small they cannot yet guess, poor things, the orphancy they are condemned to.

When in their moments of confidence these poor martyrs dare tell us their secrets, to lament their loves, always alive, to bemoan their hurts, one discovers in them such delicacy of feeling, such great treasures of tenderness (which their brave character is not enough to lessen), a selflessness so great, we involuntarily feel inferior to these anonymous and gallant heroines, who live and die attended by marvellous feats forever unknown, prodigal in miracles of love and abysmal in pardon. Stories worthy of being sung by better poets than I, and whose blessed harmonies ought to be expressed by one single note and one single chord: the chord of the sublime and the note of grief. Although lacking the strength for such a thing, nonetheless I attempted some of it in the book entitled *As viudas dos vivos e as viudas dos mortos*; but I myself recognize that I did not succeed in saying the necessary things. My strength was minimal; it needs a greater one to sing them, with all their truth and poetry, as a simple and painful epic.

Some will believe the reason for trying, as I say, to tell of things that can be described as humble, is that I express myself in our language. It is not so. Crowds of our country people will be slow reading these verses, written because of them, but only in a certain way for them. What I'd meant was to speak once more of the things of our land in our language, and to repay after a fashion the esteem and affection the *Cantares gallegos* awakened in some enthusiasts. A book of three hundred pages, written in the sweet dialect of the country, was, at that point in time, a novelty and thus past all daring. They accepted it and what is more, they did this contentedly, so I understood that from that moment I was committed not to let it be first and last. It would not do to rally the people to war and then desert the flag.

So there they go, the *Follas novas* [New Leaves], better to be styled old ones, since that is what they are; and they are last because, the debt owned my country now paid, hardly will further verse be written in the maternal tongue. There they go in search, not of triumphs, but of pardons; not of praise, but of oblivion; not of one-time predilections, but of that kindness which says of bad books, 'Let them pass!'. There, that's my wish: that it be let pass as yet another sound, as a rustic fragrance bringing along some of that poetry which, born in vast solitudes, in the permanent green countryside of our land and on the permanent beautiful beaches of our seas, seeks straightforward, natural affection in the pained hearts of this dear Galicia.

Santiago, March 30, 1880.

de *Follas novas* (1880)

Ben sei que non hai nada

Ben sei que que non hai nada
novo en baixo do ceo,
que antes outros pensaron
as cousas que hora eu penso.

E ben, ¿para qué escribo?
E ben, porque así semos,
relox que repetimos
eternamente o mesmo.

Tal coma as nubes

Tal coma as nubes
que impele o vento,
i agora asombran, i agora alegran
os espacios inmensos do ceo,
así as ideas
loucas que eu teño,
as imaxes de múltiples formas,
de estrañas feituras, de cores incertos,
agora asombran,
agora acraran,
o fondo sin fondo do meu pensamento.

from *New Leaves* (1880)

I well know there is nothing

I well know there is nothing
new under the sky,
that what I think of now
others have thought before.

Well, why do I write?
Well, because we are so,
clocks that repeat
forever the same.

As the clouds

As the clouds
borne by the wind,
now darken, now brighten
the immense spaces of the sky,
just so the mad
ideas I have,
the images of multiple forms,
of strange features, of vague colour,
now darken,
now brighten,
the abysmal depths of my mind.

Diredes de estes versos, i é verdade

Diredes de estes versos, i é verdade,
que tén estraña insólita harmonía,
que neles as ideas brillan pálidas
cal errantes muxicas
que estalan por instantes
que desparecen xiña,
que se asomellan á parruma incerta
que voltexa no fondo das curtiñas,
i ó susurro monótono dos pinos
da beiramar bravía.

Eu diréivos tan só que os meus cantares
así sán en confuso da alma miña
como sai, das profundas carballeiras,
ó comenzar do día,
romor que non se sabe
se é rebuldar das brisas,
si son beixos das frores,
si agrestes, misteriosas harmonías
que neste mundo triste
o camiño do ceo buscan perdidas.

¿Qué pasa ao redor de min?

¿Qué pasa ao redor de min?
¿Qué me pasa que eu non sei?
Teño medo dunha cousa
que vive e que non se vé.
Teño medo á desgracia traidora
que ven, e que nunca se sabe ónde ven.

You will say about these verses, and it's true

   You will say about these verses, and it's true,
that they have a strange, unusual harmony,
that in them ideas wanly glow
as straying sparks
that explode at intervals
soon vanished;
that they resemble the unsteady leaf-fall
churning in the backyards,
and the pines' monotonous sough
by the wild seashore.

   And I will tell you, my songs
issue from my soul in confusion
as out of the deep oakwoods,
at the day's start,
an indefinable hum,
maybe the chafing of the breeze,
or the kissing of flowers,
or the rustic, mysterious harmonies
that in this sad world
are at a loss to find their way to Heaven.

What's happening around me?

   What's happening around me?
What is it I do not know?
I am afraid of one thing,
something that lives yet no one sees.
I fear a treacherous fate
approaching from no one knows where.

Follas novas!, risa dame

¡Follas novas!, risa dame
ese nome que levás,
cal si a unha moura ben moura,
branca lle oise chamar.

Non *Follas novas*, ramallo
de toxos e silvas sós,
hirtas, coma as miñas penas,
feras, coma a miña dor.

Sin olido nin frescura,
bravas magoás e ferís . . .
¡Si na gándara brotades,
cómo non serés así!

Algúns din ¡miña terra!

Algúns din: ¡miña terra!
din outros: ¡meu cariño!
i este: ¡miñas lembranzas!
i aquel: ¡os meus amigos!
Todos sospiran, todos,
por algún ben perdido.
Eu só non digo nada,
eu só nunca sospiro,
que o meu corpo de terra
i o meu cansado esprito,
adonde quer que eu vaia,
vai conmigo.

New Leaves! the name you bear

New Leaves! the name you bear
makes me laugh
as if I heard someone call white
a pitch-black woman.

No *New Leaves*, a branch
of furze and brambles,
as chilling as my sorrows,
as savage as my pain.

Odourless and lifeless,
wild, you hurt and wound . . .
If you sprout in the rough land,
would you not be so!

Some people say, My country!

Some people say, My country!
Others say, My love!
And this one says, My memories!
And that one, My friends!
All, all sigh
for some lost boon.
I alone say nothing,
I alone never sigh,
since go where I may,
my earthly body,
and my weary spirit,
both follow me.

Unha vez tiven un cravo

Unha vez tiven un cravo
cravado no corazón,
i eu non me acordo xa si era aquel cravo
de ouro, de ferro ou de amor.
Soio sei que me fixo un mal tan fondo,
que tanto me atormentóu,
que eu día e noite sin cesar choraba
cal chorou Madanela na pasión.
«Señor, que todo o podedes»
— pedínlle unha vez a Dios —
«daime valor para arrincar dun golpe
cravo de tal condición.»
E doumo Dios e arrinquéino,
mais . . . ¿quen pensara? . . . Despois
xa non sentín máis tormentos
nin soupen que era delor;
soupen só que non sei que me faltaba
en donde o cravo faltou,
e seica, seica tiven soidades
daquela Pena . . . ¡Bon Dios!
Este barro mortal que envolve o esprito
¡quen o entenderá, Señor! . . .

Once I had a nail

    Once I had a nail
sunk in my heart,
a nail I can't now recall
was it gold, iron or of love.
I only know it hurt so deeply,
its torment was such
I ceaselessly mourned, day and night,
like Magdalen in the Passion.
    'Lord, you can do all things,'
I once beseeched God,
'give me the courage to pluck out with one pull
a nail so designed.'
And God obliged and I pulled it out,
but . . . who would have thought!
I felt no more torment
nor did I know pain again.
I only knew I felt a void
where the nail has been,
and I know . . . I know I longed
for that Grief . . . Good God!
This mortal clay envelops the spirit.
Who will grasp it, Lord!

Cando ún é moi dichoso, moi dichoso

Cando un é moi dichoso, moi dichoso,
¡incomprensibre arcano!,
casi que —n'e mentira anque a pareza—
lle a un pesa do ser tanto.

¡Que no fondo ben fondo das entrañas
hai un deserto páramo
que non se enche con risas nin contentos,
senón con froitos do delor amargos!

Pero cando un tén penas
i é en verdá desdichado,
oco n'atopa no ferido peito,
porque a dor ¡enche tanto!

Tan abonda é a desgracia nos seus dones
que os verte, ¡Dios llo pague!, ós regazados.
Hastra que o que os recibe,
¡ai!, reventa de farto.

When one is very, very lucky

When one is very, very lucky,
an incomprehensible secret!
so much of it — it's no lie despite appearance —
turns almost to regret.

For in one's inmost depths
there is a bleak moorland
that laughter and contentment never slake,
only the fruits of bitter pain.

Now when one pines
and is truly wretched,
no room is left in the sore breast,
for sorrow swells all.

Misfortune is so bountiful in its gifts,
these are poured even on laggards, God requite it!
Till he who receives them,
ah!, is so full that he bursts.

Hoxe ou mañán, ¿quén pode decir cándo?

Hoxe ou mañán, ¿quen pode decir cando?
Pero quisais moi logo,
viránme a despertar, i en vez dun vivo,
atoparán un morto.

Ó rededor de min levantaranse
xemidos dolorosos,
aies de angustia, choros dos meus fillos,
dos meus filliños orfos.

I eu sin calor, sin movemento, fría,
muda, insensibre a todo,
así estarei cal me deixare a morte
ó helarme co seu sopro.

E para sempre ¡adiós, canto eu quería!
¡Qué terrible abandono!
Antre cantos sarcasmos
hai, ha de haber e houbo,
non vin ningún que abata máis os vivos
que o da humilde quietú dun corpo morto.

Today or tomorrow, who can say when?

Today or tomorrow, who can say when?
But perhaps very soon,
they may come to wake me, and instead of one alive,
find someone dead.

Round about me
pain-filled howls will soar,
woes of anguish, laments of my children,
of my little orphaned children.

And I, bereft of warmth, inert, cold,
mute, insensible to all,
will stay as death has left me
frozen at its breath.

And forever, all I loved, Farewell!
What a fearsome desertion!
Amid so many sarcasms
there are, will be, and were,
I saw none depress the living more
than the humble stillness of a poor corpse.

Aquel romor de cintigas e risas

 Aquel romor de cántigas e risas,
ir, vir, algarear;
aquel falar de cousas que pasaron
i outras que pasarán;
aquela, en fin, vitalidade inquieta
xuvenil, tanto mal
me fixo, que lles dixen:
Ivos e non volvás.

 Un a un desfilaron silenciosos,
por aquí, por alá,
tal como cando as contas dun rosario
se espallan polo chan.
I o romor dos seus pasos, mentres se iñan,
de tal modo hastra min veu resoar,
que non máis tristemente
resoará quisáis
no fondo dos sepulcros
o último adios que un vivo ós mortos dá.

 I ó fin soia quedéi, pero tan soia
que hoxe da mosca o inquieto revoar,
do ratiño o roer terco e constante,
e do lume o chis chas,
cando da verde pónla
o fresco zugo devorando vai,
parece que me falan, que os entendo,
que compaña me fan;
i este meu corazón lles di tembrando:
¡Por Dios . . . non vos vaiás!

 ¡Que doce, mais que triste
tamén é a soledad!

That buzz of songs and laughter

    That buzz of songs and laughter,
going, coming, frolicking;
the telling of bygone things
and of things yet to come;
in fine, that restless,
youthful urge
hurt me so much, I said to them:
Go and don't come back.

    Silently they filed off one by one,
this way and that,
just as when so many rosary beads
are strewn about the ground.
And their footsteps' echo as they went
came to resound in me so much,
that the last farewell
the living bid the dead
is sure not to resound sadder
out of their graves' depths.

    And at last I was on my own, so alone,
that I heard the restless buzzing of the fly,
and the stubborn, ceaseless gnawing of the mouse,
the crackle of the fire
consuming
a green branch's fresh sap,
all speak to me, it seems, and I hear them,
they keep me company;
and this heart of mine tells them trembling:
Don't go, for God's sake!

    How sweet but how sad, too,
solitude is!

Xa nin rencor nin desprezo

Xa nin rencor nin desprezo,
xa nin temor de mudanzas,
tan só unha sede . . . , unha sede,
dun non sei qué que me mata.
Ríos da vida, ¿ónde estades?
¡Aire!, que o aire me falta.

— ¿Que ves nese fondo escuro?
¿Que ves que tembras e calas?
— ¡Non vexo! Miro, cal mira
un cego a luz do sol crara.
E vou caer alí en donde
nunca o que cai se levanta.

¡Silencio!

¡Silencio!
A man nerviosa e palpitante o seo,
as niebras nos meus ollos condensadas,
con un mundo de dudas nos sentidos
i un mundo de tormentos nas entrañas;
sentindo como loitan,
en sin igual batalla,
inmortales deseios que atormentan,
e rencores que matan,
mollo na propia sangre a dura pruma
rompendo a vena hinchada
i escribo . . . escribo . . . ¿para qué? ¡Volvede
ó máis fondo da ialma,
tempestosas imaxes!
¡Ide morar coas mortas relembranzas!
que a man tembrosa no papel só escriba
¡palabras, e palabras, e palabras!
¿Da idea a forma inmaculada e pura,
donde quedou velada?

Now neither rancour nor disdain

   Now neither rancour nor disdain,
nor any fear of changes,
only a thirst kills me . . . a thirst
for some unknown thing.
Rivers of life, where are you?
Air! for air fails me.

   — What do you see in that dark hollow?
What do you see to make you tremble and be silent?
— I don't see! I look as would a blind man
at the clear light of the sun.
And I'm going to fall where,
if fallen, one never rises.

Quiet!

   Quiet!
With nervous hand and beating heart,
dense mists in the eyes,
a world of doubts in the senses
and a world of torments in the innards;
feeling the unequal battle
being fought by
ever-living desires that torment,
and rancours that kill,
I moisten a hard pen in my blood
breaking the swollen vein,
and I write . . . write . . . What for? Go back
to where the soul is deepest,
stormy images!
Go dwell with dead remembrances!
Let the trembling hand on the paper only write
words, and words, and words!
The idea's neat and unblemished features:
what veils have hidden it?

¡Adios!

¡Adios!, montes e prados, igrexas e campanas,
¡adios¡, Sar e Sarela, cubertos de enramada,
¡adios!, Vidán alegre, moíños e hondanadas,
Conxo, o do craustro triste i as soedades prácidas,
San Lourenzo, o escondido, cal un niño antre as ramas,
Balvis, para min sempre o das fondas lembranzas,
Santo Domingo, en onde canto eu quixen descansa,
vidas da miña vida, anacos das entrañas.
E vós tamén, sombrisas paredes solitarias
que me vicheis chorare soia e desventurada.
¡Adiós!, sombras queridas; ¡adiós!, sombras odiadas;
outra vez os vaivéns da fertuna
pra lonxe me arrastran.

Cando volver, se volvo, todo estará onde estaba;
os mesmos montes negros i as mesmas alboradas,
do Sar i do Sarela, mirándose nas auguas.
Os mesmos verdes campos, as mesmas torres pardas
da catredal severa, ollando as lontananzas;
mais os que agora deixo, tal coma a fonte mansa
ou no verdor da vida, sin tempestás nin bágoas,
¡cánto, cando eu tornare, vítimas da mudanza,
terán de présa andado na senda da desgracia!
I eu . . . mais eu nada temo no mundo,
¡que a morte me tarda!

Goodbye!

Goodbye, mountains and meadows, churches and bells,
goodbye, Sar and Sarela, covered in bowers,
goodbye, bright Vidán, windmills and hollows,
Conxo, of the sad cloister and tranquil solitudes,
San Lourenzo, hidden like a nest in the branches,
Balvís, ever of deep-sunk memories for me,
Santo Domingo, resting-place of all I loved,
lives of my life, bits of my innards.
And you too, shadowy solitary walls
that saw me weep in loneliness and gloom.
Shadows, dear hated shadows! Goodbye, goodbye
yet again as the swings of fortune
drag me off and far away.

When, if ever, I return, all will be where it was;
the same black mountains, the same dawns,
mirrored in the waters of the Sar and the Sarela.
The same green fields, the same dark towers
of the stern cathedral, looking into the distance.
But those I leave now, gentle as the fountain,
or in the prime of life, without storms or tears,
how far, when I return, a prey to change,
will they be gone on the path of grief!
And I . . . but I fear nothing in the world,
now I find death tarrying.

Na Catedral

   Como algún día, polos corrunchos
do vasto tempro,
vellos e vellas, mentres monean,
silvan as salves i os padrenuestros;
i os arcebispos nos seus sepulcros,
reises e reinas con gran sosego
na paz dos mármores tranquilos dormen,
mentras no coro cantan os cregos.
O órgano lanza tristes cramores,
os das campanas responden lexos,
i a santa imaxe do Redentore
parés que suda sangre no Huerto.

   Señor Santisimo, ós teus pés, canto
tamén de angustia sudado teño!
Mais si o pecado castigas sempre,
ó que afrixido vai a pedircho
daille remedio.

   O sol poniente, polas vidreiras
da Soledade, lanza serenos
raios, que firen descoloridos
da Groria os ánxeles i o Padre Eterno.
Santos i apóstoles, ¡védeos!, parecen
que os labios moven, que falan quedo
os uns cos outros, e aló na altura,
do ceu a música vai dar comenzo,
pois os groriosos concertadores
tempran risoños os instrumentos.

   ¿Estarán vivos?, ¿serán de pedra
aqués sembrantes tan verdadeiros,
aquelas túnicas marabillosas,
aqueles ollos de vida cheos?

In the Cathedral

    Just any day, in the nooks
of the vast temple,
old men and women mime,
as they whisper Salves and Paternosters,
and in the tombs the archbishops,
kings and queens, all too still,
sleep in their tranquil marbles' peace,
while in the choir clergy sing.
The organ flings out sad cries,
those of the bells respond in the distance,
and the holy image of the Redeemer
seems to sweat blood in the Garden.

    Most Holy Lord, in anguish at your feet,
what I, too, didn't sweat!
But you, though you always punish sin,
you grant the remedy to the afflicted
come to beseech you.

    The setting sun, through the stained-glass windows
of the Soledad, casts gentle beams
that strike the faded angels
and the Eternal Father of Glory.
Saints and apostles, see them!
Their lips seem to move as if they spoke softly
to one another; as though high up in Heaven
music were about to start,
for the glorious concert players cheerfully
tune their instruments.

    Are they alive? Are they of stone,
these visages so true,
those marvellous tunics,
those eyes full of life?

Vós que os fixeches, de Dios c'axuda,
de inmortal nome, Mestre Mateo,
xa que aí quedaches homildemente
arrodillado, faláime deso;
mais con eses vosos cabelos rizos,
santo dos croques, calás... i eu rezo.

  Aquí está a Groria, mais naquel lado,
naquela arcada, negrexa o inferno
cas almas tristes dos condanados,
donde as devoran tódolos demos.
De alí non podo quita-los ollos,
mitá asombrada, mitá con medo,
que aqueles todos se me figuran
os dun delirio, mortaes espeutros.

  ¡Como me miran eses calabres
i aqueles deños!
¡Como me miran, facendo moecas
dende as colunas onde os puxeron!
¿Será mentira, será verdade?
Santos do ceo,
¿saberán eles que son a mesma
daqueles tempos?...
Pero xa orfa, pero enloitada,
pero insensibre cal eles mesmos...
¡Como me firen!... Voume, si, voume,
¡que teño medo!

  Mais xa nos vidros da grande araña
cai o postreiro
raio tranquilo que o sol da tarde
pousa sereno;
i en cada prancha da araña hermosa
vivos refrexos,
cintileando como as estrelas,
pintan mil cores no chan caendo,

You who made them, with God's help,
Master Mateo of undying fame:
you who here humbly
kneel, tell me of it;
but you, with your curly hair,
santo dos croques, you keep quiet . . . and I pray.

   Here is Glory, but on that side,
in that arcade, hell blackens
with the sad souls of the condemned,
where all the devils devour them.
I cannot take my eyes off them,
half astonished, half in fear,
they all strike me
as delirious, death-like spectres.

   How those cadavers
and devils look at me!
How they look at me, making faces
from the columns where they were placed!
Is it a hoax? Is it true?
Heaven's Blessed,
would they know I am the same
of former times? . . .
Only now orphaned, in mourning now,
now past feeling like themselves . . .
How they hurt me! . . . I'm off, yes, off!
For I'm afraid!

   But now the last tranquil ray
shed by the serene evening sun,
falls upon the crystals
of the great lovely chandelier
in whose every piece
vivid reflections,
sparkling like stars,
paint a thousand colours that fall on the ground,

e fan que a tola da fantesía
soñe milagres, finxa portentos.
Mais de repente veñen as sombras
todo é negrura, todo é rnisterio,
adios aixofres e marabillas . . .
tras do Pedroso púxose Febo.

  Coma pantasmas cruzan as naves
silvando salves e padrenuestros,
vellos e vellas que a Dios lle piden.
El tan só sabe cales remedios;
que cando o mundo nos deixa, é soio
cando buscamos con ansia o ceo.

  Ós pes da virxen da Soledade
— ¡de moitos anos nos conocemos! —
a oración dixen que antes dicía,
fixen mamoria dos meus secretos:
para mi madre deixéi cariños,
para os meus fillos miles de beixos,
polos verdugos do meu esprito
recei . . . ¡e funme, pois tiña medo!

De Balde

  Cando me poñan o hábito,
se é que o levo;
cando me metan na caixa,
se é que a teño;
cando o responso me canten,
se hai con que pagarlle ós cregos,
e cando dentro da cova . . .
¡Que inda me leve San Pedro
se só ó pensalo non río
con unha risa dos deños!
¡Que enterrar han enterrarme
anque non lles den diñeiro! . . .

and cause the mad fantasy
to dream miracles, feign portents.
But suddenly the shadows come
all is blackness, all is mystery.
Goodbye pearls and marvels . . .
Behind El Pedroso Phoebus just set.

    Like ghosts, the old men and women cross the aisles,
whispering Salves and Paternosters,
imploring God.
He alone knows the remedies;
it is only after the world has deserted us
we anxiously seek Heaven.

    At the feet of the Virgin of Solitude
— we've known each other for years! —
I said the prayer I used to,
I recalled my secrets:
for my mother I left affection;
a thousand kisses for my children,
I prayed for those who torment my spirit . . .
And I went off, as I was afraid!

No Charge

    When I'll be dressed in a habit,
if I'm to wear one;
when I'll be placed in the coffin
if I'm to have one;
when I'll be sung the Responso
if there's enough to pay the priests;
and when inside the tomb . . .
But may St Peter carry me off
if at the very thought I don't laugh
with the laughter of devils!
For bury me they must
though no one gives them money! . . .

Cada noite eu chorando pensaba

   Cada noite eu chorando pensaba . . .
que esta noite tan grande non fora,
que durase . . . e durase antre tanto
que a noite das penas
 me envolve loitosa.

   Mais a luz insolente do dia,
constante e traidora,
cada amañecida
penetraba radiante de groria
hastra o leito donde eu me tendera
coas miñas congoxas.

   Desde entonces busquei as tiniebras
máis negras e fondas,
e busquéinas en vano, que sempre
tras da noite topaba ca aurora . . .
So en min mesma, buscando no oscuro
i entrando na sombra,
vin a noite que nunca se acaba
na miña alma soia.

Weeping I thought each night

   Weeping I thought each night . . .
that this night were not so long
as to last . . . and last all the while,
mournful, the night of grief
surrounds me.

   But the bold light of day,
unfailing and treacherous,
gloriously radiant,
came with every dawn,
up to the bed where I had laid myself
with my anguish.

   I sought since then the blackest
and deepest darkness,
and I sought in vain, for always
after night, I met dawn . . .
Only within myself, searching in the dark
and entering the shadows,
I saw never-ending night
in my solitary soul.

¿Quén Non Xime?

   Luz e progreso en todas partes . . . pero
as dudas nos corazós,
e bágoas que un non sabe por que corren,
e dores que un non sabe por que son.

   Outro cantar, din, cansados
deste estribilo, os que chegando van
nunha nova fornada, e que andan cegos
buscando o que inda non hai.

   ¡Réprobos! . . . Sempre ó oculto perguntando
que, mudo, nada vos di.
Buscade a fe, que se perdéu na duda,
e deixá de xemir.

   Mais eles tamén perdidos
por unha i outra senda van e vén
sin que sepan, ¡coitados!, por onde andan,
sin paz, sin rumbo e sin fe.

   . . . .

   Triste é o cantar que cantamos,
mais ¿que facer si outro mellor non hai?
moita luz deslumbra os ollos,
causa inquietude o moito desear.
Cando unha peste arrebata
homes tras homes, n'hai máis
que enterrar de présa os mortos,
baixa-la frente, e esperar
que pasen as correntes apestadas . . .
¡Que pasen . . . , que outras vendrán!

Who Does Not Lament?

Light and progress everywhere . . . but
in the hearts doubts,
tears flowing no one knows why,
and regrets no one knows what for.

Another song, the fresh batch of arrivals say,
weary of the refrain,
blind they go about
in search of the non-existent.

Reprobates! . . . Always asking the hidden
that, dumb, tells you nothing.
Seek the faith you lost in doubt
and give up moaning.

But lost as well,
back and forth they tread all paths,
of their own whereabouts . . . ignorant, wretched things!
having no peace, no aim and no belief.

. . . .

The song we sing is sad,
but what to do if there is no better?
Too much light dazzles,
excessive desire disturbs.
When a plague snatches
one here, another there, nothing's left
but quickly to bury the dead,
to bend one's head, and wait
till the diseased winds pass . . .
Pass they will . . . but others will come!

¡Mar!, cas túas auguas sin fondo

¡Mar!, cas túas auguas sin fondo,
¡ceo!, ca túa inmensidá,
o fantasma que me aterra
axudádeme a enterrar.

É máis grande que vós todos
e que todos pode máis . . .
cun pé posto onde brilan os astros
e outro onde a cova me fan.

Impracabre, burlón e sañudo,
diante de min sempre vai,
i amenaza perseguirme
hastra a mesma eternidá.

Cava lixeiro, cava

Cava lixeiro, cava,
xigante pensamento,
cava un fondo burato onde a memoria
do pasado enterremos.
¡Á terra cos difuntos!
¡Cava, cava lixeiro!
E por lousa daraslle o negro olvido,
i a nada lle darás por simiterio.

Sea, with your unfathomed waters

Sea, with your unfathomed waters,
sky with your immensity,
help me bury
the ghost that frightens me.

It is greater than you both
and mightier than all . . .
one foot set where stars shine,
the other where my grave is dug.

Implacable, mocking and angry,
wherever I go it leads
and threatens to pursue me
even into eternity.

Dig fast, dig

Dig fast, dig,
giant thought,
dig a deep hollow wherein to bury
the memory of the past.
To earth with the dead!
Dig, dig fast!
And let black oblivion be the slab,
and nothingness the graveyard.

Cando penso que te fuches

Cando penso que te fuches,
negra sombra que me asombras,
ó pé dos meus cabezales
tornas facéndome mofa.

Cando maxino que es ida,
no mesmo sol te me amostras,
i eres estrela que brila,
i eres o vento que zoa.

Si cantan, es ti que cantas;
si choran, es ti que choras,
i es o marmurio do río
i es a noite i es a aurora.

En todo estás e ti es todo,
pra min i en min mesma moras,
nin me abandonarás nunca,
sombra que sempre me asombras.

When I think you are gone

When I think you are gone,
astounding black shadow,
there again by my bedside
you stand to mock me.

When I imagine you're gone,
the very sunlight reveals you,
and you are the glittering star,
and you are the chafing wind.

If they sing, it's you singing,
if they weep, it's you weeping,
and you are the river's murmur
and you are night and you are dawn.

You are in all things and you are all,
for me, even in me you dwell,
you shall never desert me,
always astounding shadow.

A Ventura é Traidora

Tembra a que unha inmensa dicha
neste mundo te sorprenda;
grorias, aquí, sobrehumanas,
tran desventuras supremas.
Nin maxines que pasan os dores
como pasan os gustos na terra;
¡hai infernos na memoria,
cando no os hai na concencia!

Cal arraigan as hedras nos muros,
nalgúns peitos arraigan as penas,
e unhas van minando a vida
cal minan outras as pedras.
Si; tembra, cando no mundo
sintas unha dicha imensa;
val máis que a túa vida corra
cal corre a iaugua serena.

Happiness is Treacherous

    Tremble at too much good luck
falling on you in this world;
here glories past the human
yield the utmost reverses.
Do not fancy griefs will pass
as do the world's pleasures.
There are the hells of memory,
should there be not those of conscience.

    As ivy grafts on the walls,
griefs strike root in some breasts,
and griefs undermine life
as roots undermine rocks.
Yes; tremble when in the world
you taste of inmense bliss;
your life had better flow
as does a tranquil stream.

Tas-tis, tas-tis, na silenciosa noite

¡Tas-tis!, ¡Tas-tis!, na silenciosa noite
con siniestro compás repite a péndola,
mentras a frecha aguda,
marcando un i outro instante antre as tiniebras,
do relox sempre imóbil
recorre lentamente a limpa esfera.
Todo é negrura en baixo,
e só na altura inmensa,
só na anchura sin límites do ceo
con inquietú relumbra algunha estrela,
cal na cinza das grandes estivadas
brilan as charamuscas derradeiras.
I a péndola no-máis, xorda batendo
cal bate un corazón que hinchan as penas,
resoa pavorosa
na escuridade espesa.
En vano a vista con temor no escuro
sin parada vaguea.
Uns tras doutros instantes silenciosos
pasando van, e silenciosos chegan
outros detrás, na eternidá caendo
cal cai o grau na moedora pedra,
sin que o porvir velado ós mortais ollos
rompa as pesadas brétemas.

¡Que triste é a noite, i o relox que triste,
si inquieto o corpo i a concencia velan!

Tick-tock, tick-tock, in the silent night

Tick-tock, tick-tock, in the silent night
with sinister beat the pendulum repeats,
while the sharp needle
marking instant after instant in the dark,
slowly circles the clean sphere
of the ever motionless clock.
Everything is black below
and only in the immense height,
only in the sky's boundless expanse
a star restlessly sparkles,
as in the ash heaps of the weed stacks
the last cinders glow.
And only the unheeding pendulum,
beats as a grief-swollen heart,
resounds awesomely
in the dense darkness.
In vain does the frightened look
obstinately scan the dark.
One after another the silent instants
pass, others silently following
to fall into eternity,
as grain falls on the mill-stone,
the future, veiled to mortal eyes,
never breaking the heavy mists.

How sad the night is, how sad the clock,
if the restless body and conscience watch!

¡Corré, serenas ondas, cristaíñas

¡Corré, serenas ondas cristaíñas,
pasade en calma e maxestosas, como
as sombras pasan dos grorioso feitos!
¡Rodade sin descanso, como rodan
á eternidá xeneraciós sin número
que cal eu vos contempro, contempráranvos!
Daime vosos perfumes, lindas rosas;
da sede que me abrasa, craras fontes,
apagade o queimor . . . nubes de gasa,
cubrí cal velo de lixeiro encaixe
do ardente sol os briladores raios.
E tí, temprada e cariñosa brisa,
dá comenzo ós concertos misteriosos,
antre os carballos da devesa escura
por onde o Sar vai marmurando leve.

O tempo pasou rápido, a centela
tal vez máis lentamente o espazo inmenso
atravesa ó caer, que eles, os anos,
pra min correron en batallas rudas . . .
¡Mais correron por fin . . . i o día chega! . . .
Dáme os teus bicos i os teus brazos ábreme
aquí, onde o río, na espesura fresca . . .
A ninguén digas onde estóu . . . con frores
das que eu quería, a delatora mancha
crube; e que nunca co meu corpo acerten
profanas mans para levarme lexos . . .
¡Quero quedar onde os meus dores foron!

Flow, serene crystal waves

Flow, serene crystal waves,
pass in calm and majesty
as do the shadows of glorious deeds!
Roll on without pause into eternity,
as did countless generations
that, like myself, gazed on you!
Give me your scents, lovely roses,
assuage, clear fountains,
the burn of the thirst that sears me . . . Gauze clouds,
cover like a veil of light lace
the brilliant rays of the burning sun.
And you, mild and caressing breeze,
commence the mysterious concerts
among the oaks of the dark range
where the Sar murmurs gently.

Time went quickly by, a spark
that falls might be slower to cross
the immense space, but for me the years
raced amid tough struggles . . .
They elapsed finely . . . and the day has come!
Give me your kisses and stretch out your arms to me,
here, by the river, in the cool thicket . . .
Tell no one where I am . . . Cover
with the flowers I've loved the betraying stain;
and let no profane hands ever find
my body to carry me faraway . . .
I want to stay where my sorrows were!

¡Qué prácidamente brilan

¡Que prácidamente brilan
o río, a fonte i o sol!
Canto brilan . . . , mais non brilan
para min, non.

¡Cal medran herbas e arbustos,
cal brota na arbor a frol!
Mais non medran, nin frorecen
para min, non.

¡Cal cantan os paxariños
enamoradas canciós!
Mais anque cantan, non cantan
para min, non.

¡Cal a natureza hermosa
sorrí a Maio que a mimou!
Mais para min non sorrí,
para min, non.

Si . . . para todos un pouco
de aire, de luz, de calor . . .
Mais si para todos hai,
para min, non.

¡E ben! . . . , xa que aquí n'atopo
aire, luz, terra, nin sol,
¿para min n'habrá unha tomba?
Para min, non.

How placid the sparkling

    How placid the sparkling
of the river, the fountain and the sun!
How they sparkle! . . . but they don't sparkle
for me, no.

    How the plants and shrubs grow,
how the flower blossoms in the tree!
But they do not grow and blossom
for me, no.

    How the birds sing
enamoured songs!
But though they sing, they do not sing
for me, no.

    How lovely Nature
smiles at May that fondled it!
But it does not smile for me,
for me, no.

    Yes . . . for everyone a little
air, light, heat . . .
But if there is that for all,
for me, no.

Well then! . . . since I cannot find
air, light, earth nor sun,
will there be no tomb for me?
for me, no.

¡Padrón!... ¡Padrón!...

¡Padrón!... ¡Padrón!...
Santa María... Lestrove...
¡Adiós! ¡Adiós!

I

Aquelas risas sin fin,
aquel brincar sin dolor,
aquela louca alegría,
¿por que acabou?
Aqueles doces cantares,
aquelas falas de amor,
aquelas noites serenas,
¿por que non son?
Aquel vibrar sonoroso
das cordas da arpa i os sons
da guitarra malencónica,
¿quen os levou?
Todo é silensio mudo,
soidá, delor,
onde outro tempo a dicha
sola reinou...

¡Padrón!... ¡Padrón!...
Santa María... Lestrove...
!Adiós! !Adiós!

II

O simiterio da Adina
n'hai duda que é encantador,
cos seus olivos escuros
de vella recordazón;
co seu chan de herbas e frores

Padrón! . . . Padrón!

Padrón! . . . Padrón!
Santa María . . . Lestrove . . .
Goodbye! Goodbye!

I

That unquelled laughter,
that carefree skipping,
that wild joy,
why did it all end?
Those sweet songs,
those words of love,
those serene nights,
why are they no more?
Those ringing chords
of the harp's strings and the sounds
of the melancholy guitar,
who snatched them off?
All is dumb silence,
solitude, grief,
where once alone
bliss reigned . . .

Padrón! . . . Padrón!
Santa María . . . Lestrove . . .
Goodbye! Goodbye!

II

The graveyard of Adina
is doubtless a delightful one,
with its sombre olive trees
remembered of old;
its ground of grass and flowers,

lindas, cal n'outras dou Dios;
co seus canónegos vellos
que nel se sentan ó sol;
cos meniños que alí xogan
contentos e rebuldós;
cas lousas brancas que o cruben,
e cos húmedos montóns
de terra, onde algunha probe
ó amañecer se enterrou.
Moito te quixen un tempo,
simiterio encantador,
cos teus olivos escuros,
máis vellos cós meus avós;
cos teus cregos venerables,
que se iban sentar ó sol,
mentras cantaban os páxaros
as matutinas cancións,
e co teu osario humilde
que tanto respeto impón
cando da luz que nel arde
vé un de noite o resprandor.
Moito te quixen e quérote,
eso ben o sabe Dios;
mas hoxe, ó pensar en ti
núbraseme o corazón:
que a terra está removida,
negra e sin frols.

Padrón! . . . Padrón!
Santa María . . . Lestrove . . .
Adios! Adios!

III

Fun un día en busca deles,
palpitante o corazón,

none lovelier God ever gave;
with the old canons
who sit there in the sun;
with children playing there
happy and romping;
studded with white slabs,
and the damp mounds of earth
where at dawn a poor one was buried.
How I loved you once,
delightful graveyard,
with your sombre olive trees,
older than my forebears;
with your venerable clergy
sitting in the sun
while the birds sang
their morning songs,
and with your humble ossuary
commanding such respect
at the nightly sight of the glow
from the lamp that lights it.
Much I have loved and
love you still, God knows;
but today, thinking of you,
my heart is overcast;
for there is fresh earth dug up,
black and bare of flowers . . .

    Padrón! . . . Padrón!
Santa María . . . Lestrove . . .
Goodbye! Goodbye!

III

    I went to find them one day,
my heart beating;

funos chamando un a un
e ningún me contestou.
Petei nunha i outra porta,
non sentín fala nin voz,
cal nunha tomba baldeira
o meu petar resonou.
Miréi pola pechadura,
¡Que silencio!... ¡que pavor!...
Vin no máis sombras errantes
que iban e viñan sin son,
cal voan os lixos leves
nun raio do craro sol.
Erguéronseme os cabelos
de estrañeza e de delor,
¡nin un soio!... ¡nin un soio!...
¿Donde están?, ¿que deles foi?
O triste son da campana,
vagoroso a min chegóu...
¡Tocaba a morto por eles!...

   ¡Padrón!... ¡Padrón!...
Santa María... Lestrove...
¡Adiós! !Adiós!

one by one I called them
and none answered me.
I knocked at door after door,
I heard no talk or voice,
as though in an empty tomb
so my knock echoed.
I looked through the keyhole.
What silence! . . .What dread! . . .
I saw only moving shades
erratically come and go,
the tiny specks that float
in a beam of the clear sun.
My hair stood on end
with shock and grief.
Not one . . . not a single one.
Where are they? Where did they go?
The sad sound of the bell,
faintly reached me . . .
It tolled for them!

Padrón! . . . Padrón!
Santa María . . . Lestrove . . .
Goodbye! Goodbye!

de *En las orillas del Sar* (1884)

Los unos, altísimos

Los unos, altísimos,
los otros, menores;
con su eterno verdor y frescura,
que inspira a las almas
agrestes canciones,
mientras gime al chocar con las aguas
la brisa marina, de aromas salobres,
van en ondas subiendo hacia el cielo
los pinos del monte.

De la altura la bruma desciende
y envuelve las copas
perfumadas, sonoras y altivas
de aquellos gigantes
que el Castro coronan;
brilla en tanto a sus pies el arroyo
que alumbra risueña
la luz de la aurora,
y los cuervos sacuden sus alas,
lanzando graznidos
y huyendo la sombra.

El viajero, rendido y cansado,
que ve del camino la línea escabrosa
que aún le resta que andar, anhelara,
deteniéndose al pie de la loma,
de repente quedar convertido
en pájaro o fuente,
en árbol o en roca.

from *On the Banks of the Sar* (1884)

Some, very high

    Some, very high,
others, lower;
forever green and fresh,
raising in the souls
rustic songs,
while the salt-scented sea breeze
moans on striking the water,
the mountain pines climb
in skyward waves.

    From on high the sea mist descends
and envelops the fragrant
peaks, sonorous and proud,
of those giants
that crown the Castro;
while the stream lit up
by dawn's gleeful light
glistens at their feet,
and the crows flutter their wings
hurling squawks
and fleeing the shade.

    The wearied, spent traveller
that watches the road's rugged stretch
still to be trodden, might wish,
as he stops at the foot of the hillock,
he were suddenly turned
into a bird or a spring,
into a tree or a rock.

Adivínase el dulce y perfumado

   Adivínase el dulce y perfumado
calor primaveral;
los gérmenes se agitan en la tierra
con inquietud en su amoroso afán,
y cruzan por los aires, silenciosos,
átomos que se besan al pasar.

   Hierve la sangre juvenil; se exalta
lleno de aliento el corazón, y audaz
el loco pensamiento sueña y cree
que el hombre es, cual los dioses, inmortal.
No importa que los sueños sean mentira,
ya que al cabo es verdad
que es venturoso el que soñando muere,
infeliz el que vive sin soñar.

   ¡Pero qué aprisa en este mundo triste
todas las cosas van!
¡Que las domina el vértigo creyérase!
La que ayer fue capullo, es rosa ya,
y pronto agostará rosas y plantas
el calor estival.

Ya duermen en su tumba a las pasiones

   Ya duermen en su tumba las pasiones
el sueño de la nada;
¿es, pues, locura del doliente espíritu,
o gusano que llevo en mis entrañas?
Yo sólo sé que es placer que duele,
que es un dolor que atormentando halaga,
llama que de la vida se alimenta,
mas sin la cual la vida se apagara.

You sense the sweet and fragrant

    You sense the sweet and fragrant
spring heat;
the seeds are stirring in the earth
with restlessness in their loving urge,
and silent atoms, that, passing, kiss,
traverse the air.

    The young blood boils, the dashing
heart soars, and the bold
mad thought dreams and believes
man is, like the gods, immortal.
No matter that dreams are lies,
since in the end it's true
that one who dies dreaming is fortunate,
and wretched, the living without dreams.

    But how fast in this sad world
all things go!
You'd think them spurred by vertigo!
What was a bud yesterday, is now a rose,
and soon the summer heat
will scorch roses and plants.

Now passions sleep in their tomb

    Now passions sleep in their tomb
dreaming of nothingness;
is it, then, madness of the grieving spirit,
or a worm I carry in my innards?
I only know it is bliss that hurts,
a hurt that by tormenting soothes,
a flame that feeds on life,
that failing, life would cease.

Un manso río, una vereda estrecha

Un manso río, una vereda estrecha,
un campo solitario y un pinar,
y el viejo puente, rústico y sencillo
completando tan grata soledad.

¿Qué es soledad? Para llenar el mundo
basta a veces un solo pensamiento,
por eso hoy, hartos de belleza, encuentras
el puente, el río y el pinar desiertos.

No son nube ni flor los que enamoran;
eres tú, corazón, triste y dichoso,
ya del dolor y del placer el árbitro,
quien seca el mar y hace habitable el polo.

Sedientas las arenas, en la playa

Sedientas las arenas, en la playa
sienten del sol los besos abrasados,
y no lejos, las ondas, siempre frescas,
ruedan pausadamente murmurando.
Pobres arenas, de mi suerte imagen:
no sé lo que me pasa al contemplaros,
pues como yo sufrís, secas y mudas,
el suplicio sin término de Tántalo.

Pero ¿quién sabe . . . ? Acaso luzca un día
en que, salvando misteriosos límites,
avance el mar y hasta vosotras llegue
a apagar vuestra sed inextinguible.
¡Y quién sabe también si, tras de tantos
siglos de ansias y anhelos imposibles,
saciará al fin su sed el alma ardiente
donde beben su amor los serafines!

A gentle river, a narrow lane

A gentle river, a narrow lane,
a solitary countryside, a pinewood,
and the old bridge, rustic and simple
completing such a pleasing solitude.

What is solitude? To fill the world
sometimes one single thought is enough,
so for a surge of beauty you find today
a deserted bridge, river and pinewood.

It's neither cloud nor flower that makes one fall in love;
it is you, heart, sad or happy,
then a judge of pain and delight,
who dries the sea and makes the Pole habitable.

Thirsting on the beach, the sands

Thirsting on the beach, the sands
feel the burning kisses of the sun,
and not faraway the waves, always fresh,
softly roll and murmur.
Poor sands, image of my fate:
something moves me at the sight of you,
for, like me, you suffer, dry and mute,
Tantalus's endless torment.

But who knows . . . ? Perhaps the day may dawn
when, overflowing mysterious rims,
the sea will rise and even reach you
to assuage your unquenchable thirst.
And who knows too if, after ages
of yearning and impossible desires,
the burning soul will at last slake its thirst
where seraphs imbibe their love!

Alma que vas huyendo de ti misma

Alma que vas huyendo de ti misma,
¿qué buscas, insensata, en las demás?
Si secó en ti la fuente del consuelo,
secas todas las fuentes has de hallar.
¡Que hay en el cielo estrellas todavía
y hay en la tierra flores perfumadas!
¡Sí! . . . Mas no son ya aquellas
que tú amaste y te amaron, desdichada.

Del antiguo camino a lo largo

Del antiguo camino a lo largo,
ya un pinar, ya una fuente aparece,
que brotando en la peña musgosa
con estrépito al valle desciende,
y brillando del sol a los rayos
entre un mar de verdura se pierde,
dividiéndose en limpios arroyos
que dan vida a las flores silvestres
y en el Sar se confunden, el río
que cual niño que plácido duerme,
reflejando el azul de los cielos,
lento corre en la fronda a esconderse.

No lejos, en soto profundo de robles,
en donde el silencio sus alas extiende
y da abrigo a los genios propicios,
a nuestras viviendas y asilos campestres,
siempre allí, cuando evoco mis sombras,
o las llamo, respóndenme y vienen.

Soul, in flight from yourself

    Soul, in flight from yourself,
what would you, stricken by folly, seek in others?
The source of solace dry within you,
you'll find all sources dry.
Are there still stars in the sky
and fragrant flowers on the earth?
Yes! . . . But they are not those, wretched one,
you loved and were loved by.

Along the ancient road

    Along the ancient road,
there rise now a pinewood, now a spring
welling up the mossy crag
and noisily streaming toward the valley;
glittering in the sun's rays,
losing itself in a sea of greenness,
parting into clear streams
that give life to the woodland flowers
and mingle in the Sar: that river,
like a child sleeping peacefully,
reflecting the sky's blue,
coursing at length to hide in the wood.

    Not far away, in the deep copse of oaks,
where silence spreads its wings
and gives cover to its propitious genii,
to our dwellings and rural shelters,
always there, when I evoke my shades
or call them, they respond and come.

Unos con la calumnia le mancharon

I

Unos con la calumnia le mancharon,
otros falsos amores le han mentido,
y aunque dudo si algunos le han querido,
de cierto sé que todos le olvidaron.

Solo sufrió, sin gloria, ni esperanza,
cuanto puede sufrir un ser viviente;
¿por qué le preguntáis qué amores siente
y no qué odios alientan su venganza?

II

Si para que se llene y se desborde
el inmenso caudal de los agravios,
quieren que nunca hasta sus labios llegue
más que el duro y amargo
pan, que el mendigo con dolor recoge
y ablanda con su llanto,
sucumbirá por fin, como sucumben
los buenos y los bravos
cuando en batalla desigual los hiere
la mano del cobarde o del tirano.

Y ellos entonces vivirán dichosos
su victoria cantando,
como el cárabo canta en su agujero
y la rana en su charco.
Mas en tanto ellos cantan . . . — ¡muchedumbre
que nace y muere en los paternos campos
siempre desconocida y siempre estéril! —
triste la patria seguirá llorando,
siempre oprimida y siempre
de la ruindad y la ignorancia pasto.

Some smeared him with slander

I

 Some smeared him with slander;
others bore him false affection;
I wonder if anyone loved him,
though I'm sure they all forgot him.

 He suffered in isolation, bereft of glory, of hope,
as much as a living being can suffer.
Why ask him what loves he feels
and not what hatreds feed his vengeance?

II

 If he wants only the hard and bitter bread
the beggar painfully picks up
and softens with his tears
to reach his lips,
so that the immense stream of wrongs
fills and overflows,
he will yield finally, as yield
the good and the brave
when in an unequal battle
the coward's or tyrant's hand wounds them.

And then they will live blest
singing their victory,
as the beetle sings in his hole
and the frog in his pool.
But while they sing . . . a throng
is born and dies in their ancestral fields,
always unknown and always sterile!
the sad native land will go on weeping,
always oppressed and always
a prey to meanness and ignorance.

En su cárcel de espinos y rosas

En su cárcel de espinos y rosas
cantan y juegan mis pobres niños,
hermosos seres, desde la cuna
por desgracia ya perseguidos.

En su cárcel se duermen soñando
cuán bello es el mundo cruel que no vieron,
cuán ancha la tierra, cuán hondos los mares,
cuán grande el espacio, qué breve su huerto.

Y le envidian las alas al pájaro
que transpone las cumbres y valles,
y le dicen: — ¿Qué has visto allá lejos,
golondrina que cruzas los aires?

Y despiertan soñando, y dormidos
soñando se quedan;
que ya son la nube flotante que pasa
o ya son el ave ligera que vuela
tan lejos, tan lejos del nido, cual ellos
de su cárcel ir lejos quisieran.

— ¡Todos parten! — exclaman. ¡Tan sólo,
tan sólo nosotros nos quedamos siempre!
¿Por qué quedar, madre; por qué no llevarnos
donde hay otro cielo, otro aire, otras gentes?

Yo, en tanto, bañados en llanto mis ojos, les miro
Y guardo silencio, pensando: — En la tierra,
¿adónde llevaros, mis pobres cautivos,
que no hayan de ataros las mismas cadenas?
Del hombre, enemigo del hombre, no puede
libraros, mis ángeles, la egida materna.

In their prison of thorns and roses

In their prison of thorns and roses
my poor children sing and play,
lovely creatures, from the cradle
hounded by grief.

Asleep in their prison they dream
how fine is the cruel world they haven't yet seen,
how broad the earth, how deep the seas,
how wide the space, their orchard how spare.

And they envy the wings of the bird
that flies over peaks and valleys,
and they say: — Swallow that crosses the sky,
far, far away, what have you seen?

And dreaming they awake, and asleep
they dream on;
and now they are the floating, passing cloud,
now the swift bird that flies off
far, as far from the nest, as they
would from their jail.

— All leave! — they exclaim. We,
we alone stay forever!
Why stay, mother; why not bring us where
there's another sky, other air, other people?

I, meanwhile, eyes bathed in tears, look at them
and keep quiet, thinking: — Where on earth
bring you, my poor captives,
so that the same chains will not bind you?
From man, man's foe, my angels,
no mother's aegis can free you.

Era la última noche

I

Era la última noche,
las noches de las tristes despedidas,
y apenas si una lágrima empañaba
sus serenas pupilas.
Como criado que deja
al amo que le hostiga,
arreglando su hatillo, murmuraba
casi con la emoción de la alegría:

— ¡Llorar! ¿Por qué? Fortuna es que podamos
abandonar nuestras humildes tierras;
el duro pan que nos negó la patria,
por más que los extraños nos maltraten,
no ha de faltarnos en la patria ajena.

Y los hijos contentos se sonríen,
y la esposa, aunque triste, se consuela
con la firme esperanza
de que el que parte ha de volver por ella.
Pensar que han de partir, ése es el sueño
que da fuerza en su angustia a los que quedan;
cuánto en ti pueden padecer, oh patria,
¡si ya tus hijos sin dolor te dejan!

II

Como a impulsos de lenta
enfermedad, hoy cien y cien mañana,
hasta perder la cuenta,
racimo tras racimo se desgrana.

It was the last night

I

It was the last night,
a night of sad goodbyes,
and scarcely a tear clouded
his calm gaze.
Like the servant about to quit
a harassing master,
he muttered almost cheerfully
while bundling his effects:

'Cry! Why? We are lucky if we can
abandon our humble patches;
however ill they treat strangers,
we won't be wanting in an alien land
the hard bread ours has refused us.'

Delighted, the children smile,
and the wife, though sad, comforts herself
in the staunch hope
the departing one will come back her rescuer.
The thought of departure, that's the dream
that lends strength in their anguish to those staying;
what your children mustn't suffer in you,
my country, if they even leave you without grief!

II

Like a prey to some slow
disease, by the hundred
until account is lost,
bunch after bunch sheds its grapes.

   Palomas que la zorra y el milano
a ahuyentar van, del palomar nativo
parten con el afán del fugitivo
y parten quizá en vano.

   Pues al posar el fatigado vuelo
acaso en el confín de otra llanura,
ven agostarse el fruto que madura,
y el águila cerniéndose en el cielo.

Camino blanco, viejo camino

Camino blanco, viejo camino,
desigual, pedregoso y estrecho,
donde el eco apacible resuena
del arroyo que pasa bullendo,
y en donde detiene su vuelo inconstante,
o el paso ligero,
de la fruta que brota en las zarzas
buscando el sabroso y agreste alimento,
el gorrión adusto,
los niños hambrientos,
las cabras monteses
y el perro sin dueño . . .
Blanca senda, camino olvidado,
¡bullicioso y alegre otro tiempo!,
del que solo y a pie, de la vida
va andando su larga jornada, más bello
y agradable a los ojos pareces
cuanto más solitario y más yermo.
Que al cruzar por la ruta espaciosa
donde lucen sus trenes soberbios
los dichosos del mundo, descalzo,
sudoroso y de polvo cubierto,
¡qué extrañeza y profundo desvío
infunde en las almas el pobre viajero!

Doves the fox and hawk
will chase, leave their native dovecote
with the migrant's care
and leave it perhaps in vain.

For perhaps on resting, their flight spent,
on the confines of some alien ground,
they see the ripening fruit wither
and the eagle hover in the sky.

White road, old road

White road, old road,
uneven, stony and narrow,
where the stream frisking by
gently echoes,
where the spare sparrow,
the hungry children,
the mountain goats
and the stray dog
halt their bouncing flight
or nimble pace
to pick the wild, rich sustenance
that grows in the bramble . . .
White path, once bustling and jolly,
now a forgotten trail,
the lonelier, the more forlorn you are,
the lovelier, the more gladdening
you look to one walking lonesome
through life's long journey.
He who barefoot and covered in dust
crosses the spacious railroad
where the world's lucky ones
display their sumptuous trains,
what an estrangement and profound aversion,
poor traveller, he instils in alien souls!

Aún parece que asoman tras el Miranda altivo

Aún parece que asoman tras del Miranda altivo,
de mayo los albores, ¡y pasó ya septiembre!
Aún parece que torna la errante golondrina,
y en pos de otras regiones ya el raudo vuelo tiende.

Ayer flores y aromas, ayer canto de pájaros
y mares de verdura y de doradas mieses;
hoy nubes que sombrías hacia Occidente avanzan,
el brillo del relámpago y el eco del torrente.

Pasó, pasó el verano rápido, como pasa
un venturoso sueño del amor en la fiebre
y ya secas las hojas en las ramas desnudas,
tiemblan descoloridas esperando la muerte.

¡Ah!, cuando en esas noches tormentosas y largas
la luna brille a intervalos sobre la blanca nieve,
¡de cuántos, que dichosos ayer la contemplaron,
alumbrarán la tumba sus rayos transparentes!

Muda la luna, y como, siempre pálida

Muda la luna y como siempre pálida,
mientras recorre la azulada esfera
seguida de su séquito
de nubes y de estrellas,
rencorosa despierta en mi memoria
yo no sé qué fantasmas y quimeras.

Y con sus dulces misteriosos rayos
derrama en mis entrañas tanta hiel,
que pienso con placer que ella, la *eterna*,
ha de pasar también.

It seems that, behind proud Miranda, they still loom

It seems that, behind proud Miranda, they still loom,
May's dawnlights, yet now September's over!
It seems that the migrant swallow returns,
yet now its swift flight is set for other places.

Yesterday flowers and scents, yesterday birdsong
and seas of verdure and golden corn fields;
today dark clouds that move Westward;
the lightning's flash and the creek's echo.

Fleet summer passed, as does
some happy dream of love in a fever;
and now on the bare branches the dry leaves
quiver, discoloured, awaiting death.

Ah, when on the long and stormy nights
by spells the moon shines on the white snow,
of those who were yesterday lucky to watch it,
whose tomb will its clear rays light up?

The moon, silent and, as always, pale

The moon, silent and, as always, pale,
while traversing the bluish sphere
followed by her retinue
of clouds and stars,
rancourously stirs in my memory
I know not what ghosts and chimeras.

And with its sweet mysterious rays
she so soaks in bile my innards,
I revel in the thought that she, though *eternal*,
shall also pass.

Una sombra tristísima, indefinible y vaga

Una sombra tristísima, indefinible y vaga
como lo incierto, siempre ante mis ojos va
tras de otra vaga sombra que sin cesar la huye,
corriendo sin cesar.
Ignoro su destino . . . , mas no sé por qué temo
al ver su ansia mortal,
que ni han de parar nunca, ni encontrarse jamás.

Cuando sopla el Norte duro

Cuando sopla el Norte duro
y arde en el hogar el fuego,
y ellos pasan por mi puerta
flacos, desnudos y hambrientos,
el frío hiela mi espíritu,
como debe helar su cuerpo,
y mi corazón se queda
al verlos ir sin consuelo,
cual ellos, opreso y triste,
desconsolado cual ellos.

Era niño y ya perdiera
la costumbre de llorar;
la miseria seca el alma
y los ojos además;
era niño y parecía
por sus hechos, viejo ya.

Experiencia del mendigo,
era precoz como el mal,
implacable como el odio,
dura como la verdad.

The saddest shadow, indefinable and vague

The saddest shadow, indefinable and vague,
like doubtful things, moves always before my eyes,
ceaseless pursuer of a shadow
in ceaseless flight.
Their intent is closed to me . . . , but I fear I don't know why
on seeing their deadly greed,
they will never halt, nor ever meet.

When the harsh Northwind blows

When the harsh Northwind blows
and a fire burns in the hearth
and they pass by my door,
thin, naked and hungry,
the cold freezes my spirit
as it must freeze their body,
and on seeing them go
unconsoled, my heart's left,
like them, sad and oppressed,
disconsolate like them.

He was a child, yet one lost
to the habit of tears;
need dries up the soul
and also the eyes;
he was a child, one who appeared
by his deeds already old.

A beggar's experience,
it was precocious as evil,
implacable as hatred,
tough as truth.

Dicen que no hablan las plantas, ni las fuentes, ni los pájaros

Dicen que no hablan las plantas, ni las fuentes, ni los pájaros,
ni la onda con sus rumores, ni con su brillo los astros;
lo dicen, pero no es cierto, pues siempre cuando yo paso
de mí murmuran y exclaman:
                        — Ahí va la loca, soñando
la eterna primavera de la vida y de los campos,
y ya bien pronto, bien pronto, tendrá los cabellos canos,
y ve temblando, aterida, que cubre la escarcha el prado.

— Hay canas en mi cabeza, hay en los prados escarcha;
mas yo prosigo soñando, pobre, incurable sonámbula,
con la eterna primavera de la vida que se apaga
y la perenne frescura de los campos y las almas,
aunque los unos se agostan y aunque las otras se abrasan.

Astros y fuentes y flores, no murmuréis de mis sueños;
sin ellos, ¿cómo admiraros, ni cómo vivir sin ellos?

Some say plants don't speak, nor fountains, nor birds

   Some say plants don't speak, nor fountains, nor birds,
nor the wave with its swish, nor stars with their sparkle:
so say some, but it isn't true, since always as I pass by,
things whisper about me and exclaim:
                        — There goes the madwoman, dreaming
of the eternal spring of life and the fields,
though soon enough, all too soon, she will comb grey hair,
and shivering, numb, see the hoarfrost shroud the meadow.

   — There's white hair on my head, hoarfrost in the meadows;
but I, poor soul, incurable sleepwalker, dream on and on
of expiring life's eternal spring
and the perennial freshness of fields and souls
even though these burn up and those wither.

   Stars and fountains and flowers, don't murmur against my dreams;
could I delight in you without them, without them, could I live?

¡Pensamientos de alas negras!, huid, huid azorados

¡Pensamientos de alas negras!, huid, huid azorados,
como bandada de cuervos por la tormenta acosados,
o como abejas salvajes en quien el fuego hizo presa;
dejad que amanezca el día de resplandores benditos
en cuya luz se presienten los placeres infinitos . . .
¡y huid con vuestra perenne sombra que en el alma pesa!

¡Pensamientos de alas blancas!, ni gimamos ni roguemos
como un tiempo, y en los mundos luminosos penetremos
en donde nunca resuena la débil voz del caído,
en donde el dorado sueño para en realidad segura,
y de la humana flaqueza sobre la inmensa amargura
y sobre el amor que mata, sus alas tiende el olvido.

Ni el recuerdo que atormenta con horrible pesadilla,
ni la pobreza que abate, ni la miseria que humilla,
ni de la injusticia el látigo, que al herir mancha y condena,
ni la envidia y la calumnia más que el fuego asoladoras
existen para el que siente que se deslizan sus horas
del contento y la abundancia por la corriente serena.

Allí, donde nunca el llanto los párpados enrojece,
donde por dicha se ignora que la humanidad padece
y que hay seres que codician lo que harto el perro desdeña;
allí, buscando un asilo, mis pensamientos dichosos
a todo pesar ajenos, lejos de los tenebrosos
antros del dolor, cantemos a la esperanza risueña.

Frescas voces juveniles, armoniosos instrumentos,
¡venid!, que a vuestros acordes yo quiero unir mis acentos
vigorosos, y el espacio llenar de animadas notas,
y entre estatuas y entre flores, entrelazadas las manos,
danzar en honor de todos los venturosos humanos
del presente, del futuro y las edades remotas.

Black-winged thoughts! flee, flee harass-ridden

Black-winged thoughts! flee, flee harass-ridden,
like flocks of ravens harried by the storm,
or like wild bees preyed on by fire;
let day dawn amid blissful splendours,
in whose light endless joys are sensed . . .
and flee with your perennial soul-crushing shadow!

White-winged thoughts! let us not wail or pray
as once, and let us enter the luminous worlds,
where the weak voice of the fallen never rings,
where the golden dream turns assured reality
and oblivion spreads its wings over human frailty's
immense bitterness and the love that kills.

Nor the memory that haunts like a terrible nightmare,
nor the poverty that bends, nor the want that humiliates,
nor the injustice of the lash, that, striking, soils and damns,
nor envy and slander, more ravaging than fire,
exist for one who feels his hours of contentment
and bounty slipping by in the quiet stream.

There where weeping never reddens the eyelids,
where there is lucky ignorance that humanity suffers
and that there are some who covet what the replete dog rejects;
there, in search of shelter, happy thoughts of mine,
alien to all regret, far from the tenebrous
caverns of grief, let us sing to smiling hope.

Fresh young voices, harmonious instruments,
come!, for I want my vigorous accents to join
your tunes, and to fill space with lively notes,
dancing amid statues and flowers, hands
entwined, in honour of all happy humans
of the present, the future and long gone ages.

Son los corazones de algunas criaturas

Son los corazones de algunas criaturas
como los caminos muy transitados,
donde las pisadas de los que ahora llegan
borran las pisadas de los que pasaron:
no será posible que dejéis en ellos,
de vuestro cariño, recuerdo ni rastro.

La palabra y la idea . . . Hay un abismo

La palabra y la idea . . . Hay un abismo
entre ambas cosas, orador sublime;
si es que supiste amar, di: cuando amaste,
¿no es verdad, no es verdad que enmudeciste?
Cuando has aborrecido, ¿no has guardado
silencioso, la hiel de tus rencores
en lo más hondo y escondido y negro
que hallar puede en sí un hombre?

Un beso, una mirada,
suavísimo lenguaje de los cielos;
un puñal afilado, un golpe aleve,
expresivo lenguaje del infierno.
Mas la palabra en vano
cuando el odio o el amor llenan la vida,
al convulsivo labio balbuciente
se agolpa y precipita.
¡Qué ha de decir! Desventurada y muda,
de tan hondos, tan íntimos secretos,
la lengua humana, torpe, no traduce
el velado misterio.
Palpita el corazón enfermo y triste,
languidece el espíritu, he aquí todo;
después se rompe el frágil
vaso, y la esencia elévase a lo ignoto.

The hearts of some creatures

The hearts of some creatures
are like well-trodden roads,
where the footsteps of those who come
erase the steps of those who went:
you won't manage to leave there
remembrance or trace of your affection.

The word and the idea . . . There is an abyss

The word and the idea . . . There is an abyss
between both things, sublime orator;
if you learn to love, tell me: when you loved,
is it not true, is it not true you were struck dumb?
When you have hated, did you not, silent,
keep the bile of your rancours
in the deepest, remotest and blackest place
to be found by a man in his innards?

A kiss, a look,
heaven's gentlest language;
a sharp dagger, a base blow,
the eloquent language of hell.
But when hate or love fill life,
in vain the word
swells and rushes
to the convulsed, halting lip.
What would it say? Wretched and mute
man's inept tongue cannot spell
the veiled mystery
of such deep, such intimate secrets.
Sad and sick the heart beats,
the spirit pines, that is all;
then the frail vase breaks
and its scent soars to the unknown.

«Los muertos van de prisa»

«Los muertos van de prisa»,
el poeta lo ha dicho;
van tan de prisa, que sus sombras pálidas
se pierden del olvido en los abismos
con mayor rapidez que la centella
se pierde en los espacios infinitos.

«Los muertos van de prisa»; mas yo creo
que aún mucho más de prisa van los vivos.
¡Los vivos!, que con ansia abrasadora,
cuando apenas vivieron
un instante de gloria, un solo día
de júbilo, y mucho antes de haber muerto,
unos a otros sin piedad se entierran
para heredarse presto.

De este mundo en la comedia

De este mundo en la comedia
eterna, vienen y van
bajo un mismo velo envueltas
la mentira y la verdad;
por eso al verlas el hombre
tras del mágico cendal
que vela la faz de entrambas,
nunca puede adivinar
con certeza cuál es de ellas
la mentira o la verdad.

'The dead go fast'

'The dead go fast,'
the poet said;
they go so fast, their pale ghosts
vanish in oblivion's gulfs
faster than the spark
vanishes in boundless space.

'The dead go fast,' but I think
the living go faster yet.
The living! who burnt by greed,
when they have scarcely lived
an instant of glory, a single day
of joy, and long before they're dead,
unpityingly bury each other
for a fast inheritance.

In this world's endless

In this world's endless
comedy, both shrouded
by the one same veil,
truth and lie come and go;
so man, that sees them
under the magic gauze
veiling the face of both,
in certitude cannot tell
which of the two is which,
neither the lie nor the truth.

Las Campanas

   Yo las amo, yo las oigo
cual oigo el rumor del viento,
el murmurar de la fuente
o el balido del cordero.

   Como los pájaros, ellas,
tan pronto asoma en los cielos
el primer rayo del alba,
le saludan con sus ecos.

   Y en sus notas, que van repitiéndose
por los llanos y los cerros,
hay algo de candoroso,
de apacible y de halagüeño.

   Si por siempre enmudecieran,
¡qué tristeza en el aire y en el cielo!,
¡qué silencio, en las iglesias!
¡qué extrañeza entre los muertos!

The Bells

I love them, I hear them
as I hear the sound of the wind,
the murmur of the fountain
or the bleat of the lamb.

As soon as the first dawn ray
appears in the sky, they,
like the birds,
greet it with their echoes.

And in their notes that carry
over the plains and hills,
there is a touch of candour,
something gentle and encouraging.

Were they forever silent,
what sadness to the air and sky!,
what silence in the churches!
what astonishment among the dead!

En la altura los cuervos graznaban

En la altura los cuervos graznaban,
los deudos gemían en torno del muerto,
y las ondas airadas mezclaban
sus bramidos al triste concierto.

Algo había de irónico y rudo
en los ecos de tal sinfonía;
algo negro, fantástico y mudo
que del alma las cuerdas hería.

Bien pronto cesaron los fúnebres cantos,
esparcióse la turba curiosa,
acabaron gemidos y llantos
y dejaron al muerto en su fosa.

Tan sólo a lo lejos, rasgando la bruma,
del negro estandarte las orlas flotaron,
como flota en el aire la pluma
que al ave nocturna los vientos robaron.

¡Justicia de los hombres!, yo te busco

Justicia de los hombres, yo te busco,
pero sólo te encuentro
en la palabra, que tu nombre aplaude,
mientras te niega tenazmente el hecho.

— Y tú, ¿dónde resides — me pregunto
con aflicción —, justicia de los cielos,
cuando el pecado es obra de un instante
y durará la expiación terrible
mientras dure el Infierno?

High up the ravens croaked

High up the ravens croaked,
the kin wailed round the dead man,
and the angry waves blended
their roar with the sad concert.

There was something ironic and crude
in the echoes of such a symphony;
something black, fantastic and mute
that struck the chords of the soul.

Soon enough the funereal songs ceased,
the curious throng dispersed,
the moans and groans ended
and the dead man was left in his grave.

Alone in the distance, tearing the mist,
the borders of the black banner floated,
as would the air-borne feather
the winds robbed of a night bird.

Justice of men, I seek you out

Justice of men, I seek you out,
only to find you
in the word, that hails your name,
while the stubborn fact belies you.

— And you? Where do you dwell? — I ask myself
in pain—, justice of heavens,
when sin is an instant's thing
and dire atonement lasts
all the while Hell must last.

Al caer despeñado en la hondura

Al caer despeñado en la hondura
desde la alta cima,
duras rocas quebraron sus huesos,
hirieron sus carnes agudas espinas,
y el torrente de lecho sombrío,
rasgando sus linfas
y entreabriendo sus húmedos labios,
vino a darle un beso de muerte
cerrando en los suyos el paso a la vida.

Despertáronle luego, y temblando
de angustia y de miedo,
— ¡Ah!, ¿por qué despertar? — preguntóse
después de haber muerto.

Al pie de su tumba
con violados y ardientes reflejos,
flotando en la niebla
vio dos ojos brillantes de fuego,
que al mirarle ahuyentaban el frío
de la muerte templando su seno.

Y del yermo sin fin de su espíritu
ya vuelto a la vida, rompiéndose el hielo,
sintió al cabo brotar en el alma
la flor de la dicha, que engendra el deseo.
Dios no quiso que entrase infecunda
en la fértil región de los cielos;
piedad tuvo del ánima triste
que el germen guardaba de goces eternos.

As from the high summit

    As from the high summit
he fell off a cliff into the deep,
hard rocks smashed his bones,
sharp thorns hurt his flesh;
and the dark-bedded torrent
tearing its lymphs,
its moist lips parting in a black smile
offered him the kiss of death,
his lips in turn locked on to life.

    Then they woke him, and trembling
in anguish and fear,
—Ah! why awake — he asked,
after one is dead?

    Beside his grave,
adrift in the mist,
amid violet and flame-like flashes,
he saw the glint of two fiery eyes
that made death's cold recede
and his breast warm up.

    And the ice cracking in the boundless desert
of his spirit now come back to life,
he felt at last the flower of bliss
that arouses desire, bud in the soul.
God would not have it trodden barren
the fertile regions of heavens;
he took pity on the sad wraith
that hid the seed of eternal joys.

Yo no he nacido para odiar, sin duda

¡No! No ha nacido para amar, sin duda,
ni tampoco ha nacido para odiar,
ya que el amor y el odio han lastimado
su corazón de una manera igual.

Como la dura roca
de algún arroyo solitario al pie,
inmóvil y olvidado, anhelaría
ya vivir sin amar ni aborrecer.

Aunque no alcancen gloria

Aunque no alcancen gloria,
pensé, escribiendo libro tan pequeño,
son fáciles y breves mis canciones,
y acaso alcancen mi anhelado sueño.
Pues bien puede guardarlas la memoria
tal como, pese al tiempo y la distancia,
y al fuego asolador de las pasiones,
sabe guardar las que aprendió en la infancia,
cortas, pero fervientes oraciones.
Por eso son, aunque no alcancen gloria,
tan fáciles y breves mis canciones.

Doubtless, he wasn't born to love, no

    Doubtless, he wasn't born to love, no;
nor was he born to hate,
for love and hate have
alike wounded his heart.

    As the hard rock
by some solitary stream,
unstirring and forgotten,
would now live neither loving nor hating.

Although they may not achieve glory

    Although they may not achieve glory,
I thought, writing such a small book,
my songs are easy and short,
and perhaps they may achieve my longed-for dream.
Well can memory keep them,
since, despite time and distance
and the ravaging fire of passions,
it retains the prayers, brief and fervent,
learned in childhood.
Hence these songs so easy and short,
though they may not achieve glory.

Hora tras hora, día tras día

Hora tras hora, día tras día,
entre el cielo y la tierra que quedan
eternos vigías,
como torrente que se despeña
pasa la vida.

Devolvedle a la flor su perfume
después de marchita;
de las ondas que besan la playa
y que una tras otra besándola expiran
recoged los rumores, las quejas,
y en planchas de bronce grabad su armonía.

Tiempos que fueron, llantos y risas,
negros tormentos, dulces mentiras,
¡ay!, ¿en dónde su rastro dejaron,
en dónde, alma mía?

Hour after hour, day after day

    Hour after hour, day after day,
between enduring heaven and earth,
eternal lookouts,
life passes
like a hurtling torrent.

    Give back to the flower its fragrance
after it withers;
gather the sounds, the plaints
of the waves that in succession
kiss the shore and die,
and carve their harmony on bronze sheets.

    Times that were, laments and laughter,
black torments, sweet lies,
ah, my soul! where,
where did they leave their trace?

Era apacible el día

Era apacible el día
y templado el ambiente
y llovía, llovía
callada y mansamente;
y mientras silenciosa
lloraba yo y gemía,
mi niño, tierna rosa,
durmiendo se moría.

Al huir de este mundo, ¡qué sosiego en su frente!
Al verle yo alejarse, ¡qué borrasca en la mía!

Tierra sobre el cadáver insepulto
antes que empiece a corromperse . . . , ¡tierra!
Ya el hoyo se ha cubierto, sosegaos;
bien pronto en los terrones removidos
verde y pujante crecerá la hierba.

¿Qué andáis buscando en torno a las tumbas,
torvo el mirar, nublado el pensamiento?
¡No os ocupéis de lo que al polvo vuelve!
Jamás el que descansa en el sepulcro
ha de tornar a amaros ni a ofenderos.

¡Jamás! ¿Es verdad que todo
para siempre acabó ya?
No, no puede acabar lo que es eterno,
ni puede tener fin la inmensidad.

Tú te fuiste para siempre; mas mi alma
te espera aún con amoroso afán,
y vendrás o iré yo, bien de mi vida,
allí donde nos hemos de encontrar.

The day was mild

The day was mild
and the air gentle,
and it rained, it rained
quietly and gently;
and while I silently
wept and moaned,
my child, a tender rose,
died in its sleep.

On leaving this world, what joy on his brow!
Seeing him depart, what a storm on mine!

Earth above the unburied corpse
before it begins to decompose . . . earth!
Be calm, already the hollow has been filled in;
soon enough grass will grow
green and strong in the upturned clods.

What are you seeking around the graves,
grimly gazing, your thought overcast?
Don't worry about what reverts to dust!
Who rests in the grave
can never come back to love or offend you.

Never! Is it true that everything
is forever ended then?
No, what is eternal can never end,
immensity can have no finish.

You went away forever; but my soul
is still waiting for you with devoted longing,
and you will come and I will go, love of my life,
there where we must meet.

Algo ha quedado tuyo en mis entrañas
que no morirá jamás,
y que Dios, porque es justo y porque es bueno,
a desunir ya nunca volverá.

En el cielo, en la tierra, en lo insondable
yo te hallaré y me hallarás.
No, no puede acabar lo que es eterno,
ni puede tener fin la inmensidad.

Mas . . . es verdad, ha partido,
para nunca más tornar.
Nada hay eterno para el hombre, huésped
de un día en este mundo terrenal
en donde nace, vive y al fin muere,
cual todo nace, vive y muere acá.

Something of yours stayed in my innards,
that will never die,
and that God, because he is just and good,
will never separate.

In the sky, in the earth, in the unfathomable
I will find you and you will find me.
No, what is eternal can never end,
immensity can have no finish.

But . . . it's true, he has left
never again to return.
There is nothing eternal for man, a guest
for a day in this terrestrial world
where he is born, lives and finally dies,
as everything here is born, lives and dies.

Women Writers

A Letter to Eduarda

My dear Eduarda: Shall I be cruel at the beginning of this letter by telling you that your last one made me feel sad and put me out of humour? Shall I continue to seem to you envious of your talents, or, being brutally frank, dare to despoil you, patently and pitilessly, of those dear interests that you caress with so much passion? But you know who I am; you know my feelings so intimately, my heartfelt affections, that it is possible for me to speak to you.

No, a thousand times no, Eduarda. Distance yourself from such a fatal temptation, publish nothing and keep for yourself alone your verses, your prose, your novels and your plays. Let that be a secret between heaven and us two. Do you not see that the world is full of these things? Everyone writes, and writes about everything. The Muses have been let loose. There are more books than the sea has sand, more geniuses than the sky has stars, and more critics than the fields have grass. Many have taken up this last occupation and are rewarded for it with the praises of the Fatherland, and although they do the worst that can be expected of them, they enthusiastically persist, laughing, inanely happy, at other fools while the rest laugh at them. Like a devastating plague, critics and writers have invaded the earth and do their best to devour it. What need is there of you and me in this devastating confusion? None. And what is not needed is always idle. You will say that I am treating this question like that of marriage about which we speak badly after having got married. But I can assure you, my dear friend, that if marriage for us is almost a necessity imposed by society and Nature, the Muses are a cliff and nothing more. And, anyway, do they deserve to be loved? Have they not become so crude and vulgar, they turn up for the first that calls on them, even for one with a wholly vacant head? Judge by what I am going to tell you.

Some time ago my husband's barber presented himself

cautiously and yet with a haughty seriousness. Having bumped into the cook on entering, he stretched out his hand and greeted her courteously.

— 'At your feet, María. How is your health?' —

— 'We're getting on,' she said laughing. — 'And what about you, Guanito?'

— 'I'm fine, thanks, and at your service'.

— 'How very thoughtful, my dear friend!', she added, thinking herself raised to the fifth heaven, because the little barber had given her his hand in greeting and had placed himself at her service. — 'How obvious it is you have lived in Havana! Here, young men scarcely know how to say 'Good day!'

— 'One knows at once you come from those parts . . .' — I said to myself. You know, Eduarda, what those parts are . . . that happy region where all, all (I believe even the spiders) descend in a direct line from a certain, ancient, ingenious and artistic race that taught the world its art and wisdom.

— 'Why weren't you here before?' my husband asked him rather seriously. — 'Don't you know I was waiting for you since ten?'

— 'Everyone has his own private concerns,' the barber answered in a heavy tone while he toyed with his cane. — 'I had to finish my book and bring it to the printer's in time.'

— 'What book?' my husband responded with great surprise.

— 'A novel, moral, instructive and scientific, which I have just written and in which I palpably demonstrate that of a barber's is the most interesting of all the occupations that are termed mechanic, and should be raised to the status of an honorable and titled profession, and, moreover, transcendental.'

My husband got up then from the chair where he sat, ready be butchered; and picking up some coins he handed them over to the barber, saying, — 'By God, you are doing such work, that it is not fitting you should shave my face' — and he went off laughing obstreperously. But not so myself, irritated as I was by the stupidity of the Muses. I opened my folder and minced all the writing I had in it, an action by which, truth to tell, nothing has been lost.

For such is the world, Eduarda: it will take that barber's book, the monster hatched by someone God made thick as a marmot, who may well compare it with a novel by George Sand.

— 'I have read many charming books,' a young man of some education once said to me. 'Evenings in La Granja and Byron's Manfred. But most of all, Evenings in la Granja made me happy.'

— 'I believe so,' I answered, and changed the topic.

It is intolerable for someone who has some literary pride and some feeling for poetry in one's heart; but above all, my dear friend, you do not know what it is to be a woman writer. Being one like George Sand is some worth; if that isn't the case, what a ceaseless torment! They constantly point you out in the street, and not to any good, and you are everywhere the butt of gossip. If you go to a tertulia to discuss something you know, if you merely express yourself somewhat correctly, they call you a *bachillera*, they say you are listening to yourself, that you want to know everything. If you maintain a prudent reserve, how fatuous! how conceited!; you think it below yourself to converse save with the learned. If you keep a low profile, so you avoid getting into futile disputes, you are allowing challenging questions to pass unnoticed, where is your talent? you don't even know how to amuse people with entertaining conversation. If society attracts you, you are trying to show off, you want to be spoken about, no occasion is free of some bugbear. If you forego intercourse with other people, it is to make yourself interesting, you are mad, your character is morose and insufferable; you spend your days in poetic swoons and your nights contemplating the stars like Don Quijote. Women exaggerate your defects and men skip no opportunity to tell you that a woman of talent is a true calamity, that it is more rewarding to marry the ass of Balaam, and that only a silly wife can make a mortal *varón* happy.

Above all, those who write and consider themselves witty, never let an opportunity pass without telling you that women should put aside the pen and mend the socks of the husband, if they have one, and if not, then those of the servant. It would be easy for some women to open the wardrobe and deposit, so the husband would bump on it, the patiently worked darning, thus showing him that to write some pages does not cause them to forget their home chores, adding perhaps that the grumblers in their turn forget they were born for something beyond gobbling the day's bread and living as parasites.

But the fact is, Eduarda, men look on women writers as worse than they would the Devil; and this is yet another reef you ought to fear, you who have no dowry. Only, someone of real talent, assessing your worth, would despise foolish and erroneous prejudices; but . . . woe be you then! none of what you write is yours, your estrus is at an end, your husband's the writer and you merely sign your name.

I, whom doubtless an evil jinnee chose to set on the perverse road of the Muses, know all too well the path we walk on such pilgrimage. In regard to myself, it is said as a matter of course that my husband is toiling incessantly to make me immortal. Verse, prose, good or bad, all is his, but particularly whatever appears to them not so bad, and no one, whether poetry freshman or brainy senior, disagrees there. So they blame him for sins he has not committed! An annoying prejudice, a painful task, certainly, is that of my husband, already at great pains to write his own stuff (lazy as most poets are), who is supposed to write his wife's books as well, which means no doubt that what he has for a wife is a poetess (a word that has hurt me), or a novelist, that is, the worst thing a woman can be in our day.

It is rather absurd on reflection, and it even seems the opposite of the good taste and refinement of a man and a woman who are not absolutely stupid . . . But how to believe that she can write such things? A woman whom they see every day, whom they know since she was a child, whom they have heard speaking, and indeed not in Andalusian but straightforward and plain as anyone, can she discuss and write things that have never crossed the minds of those who have studied and know philosophy, law, rhetoric and poetics, etc? Impossible! Not to be believed, unless God comes down to tell it. If she had at least been born in France or in Madrid! But here? . . . Oh! . . .

All this in general matters little to me, Eduarda, yet there are times when it offends me and hurts my self-esteem, and here's another torment you must add to those already mentioned.

But do not think the ill rests at that, for a poetess or woman writer will not enjoy human peace on this earth, since in addition to her spirit's troubles, she must face many another, raised on all sides by those around her.

If you marry a common man, even one who torments you and oppresses you day and night, giving you no respite, to the world you are the one handling him, the one pulling him this way and that, the one ruling him; when visiting he recites the lesson you have taught him at home, and he'd dare not raise his eyes for fear you'll scold him, and all this results in contempt for your husband, it cannot but wound you mortally if you have feelings and dignity, because the first thing a woman has to take care of is that the dignity and honour of her husband may rank as high as possible. Any stain that falls on him spreads to you and your children; that is the column on which you rest and it doesn't wobble without yourself wobbling too, nor can it be overthrown without it dragging you down in its fall.

There, hastily sketched out and at great risk, the life of a woman writer. Read and reflect. I eagerly await your reply.

Your friend, Nicanora.

Strolling one day round and about the outskirts of town, I found a wallet that contained this letter. Not because of its literary merit, rather for the motive that urged the writer, I deemed it so much in accord with my taste, I felt encouraged to make it public. I trust the unknown sender, reassured of the affinity of our feelings, will pardon me this liberty.